Religious Imagination

RELIGIOUS IMAGINATION

God's Gift to Prophets and Preachers

By
ROBERT D. YOUNG

THE WESTMINSTER PRESS
Philadelphia

BOOK DESIGN BY DOROTHY ALDEN SMITH

First edition

Published by The Westminster Press ®
Philadelphia, Pennsylvania

PRINTED IN THE UNITED STATES OF AMERICA

9 8 7 6 5 4 3 2 1

Library of Congress Cataloging in Publication Data

Young, Robert Doran, 1928–
Religious imagination.

Includes bibliographical references.
1. Clergy—Office. 2. Imagination. 3. Crea-
tion (literary, artistic, etc.) 4. Identification
(Religion) I. Title.
BV660.Y68   253   78–26843
ISBN 0–664–24239–1

Contents

Acknowledgments

Few accomplishments in life are achieved solely on one's own.

I would like to identify some of the help I received in the production of this book. The prodding force came from an editor and friend, Dr. Roland W. Tapp, whose constant encouragement kept me going. The germinal thought and time to begin came at the Princeton Summer Institute of '76, where a fine program, plus an out-of-the-way room in the library, was a great stimulation to concentrated work.

Two close friends, members of my congregation, gave many suggestions for bibliography. They are Dr. Arthur C. Eckerman and Mr. Robert Dale McKinney, both professors at West Chester State College and both highly creative men, one in business administration and one in art.

Needless to say, my experience in the parish ministry provided raw material for the book. My indebtedness to the people of the Woodland Avenue Presbyterian Church of Philadelphia and the Westminster Presbyterian Church of West Chester, Pennsylvania, can scarcely be repaid.

Then, finally, I pay tribute to my wife, who acts as critic, proofreader, and stimulator of ideas.

However, I do not want to blame the book on any of the above, for I would like to keep my friends for a long while to come, and also to remain happily married.

IDENTITY CRISIS
IN THE PULPIT

The identity crisis of a minister in the late twentieth century is serious and disconcerting. Being a minister, and one who places stronger emphasis on the pulpit than other areas, I have felt this crisis intensely. Who am I? What is my function? What is at the essence of what I do? When I reach retirement will someone paraphrase Arthur Miller: "Poor Rev. Loman, he didn't know who he was"?

In former generations, a minister was proud to be called "the Preacher." However, modern ministers resist such a label. Either it conjures up an image of a Victorian man in a winged collar and cutaway coat, a prince of the pulpit; or it emphasizes the mouth at a time when most problems are handled by intense listening, or keen thinking, or aggressive doing. Neither connotation of the title "Preacher" fits comfortably around ministers who search for identity. In fact, almost any other designation seems preferable: administrator, educator, prophet, theologian, writer, counselor, etc. Most ministers prefer to choose one or several titles, and find their life's meaning in the structure of connotations. Yet the malaise lingers. None of these titles really touches the root of the matter. In moments of quiet self-examination, the question "Who am I?" still appears out of nowhere to disturb the solitude.

What adds to the problem of identity is the not-so-subtle pressures to define ourselves in business terms. The Willy Loman of *Death of a Salesman* was trying to make it in sales, and modern ministers often wonder if that does not say it all. We are always pushing something: the latest program, the new building, next year's budget, the church officers' retreat, the summer camp, the community festival. We might protest materialism and success-oriented goals, but inadvertently we all succumb while sitting behind our Madison Avenue desks. The walls of our minds are papered with graphs and charts showing increases or decreases of members and money. Unconsciously we ask: What are the trends? Where is the market? How can we capture more of the market from our "competitors"? Who are our potential "customers"? The questions, all of which proceed from the business mentality, surround the clergy like a thicket, and are just as difficult to get through. On the one hand, after asking them uncritically, we feel guilty if we can't give good answers that will satisfy the board. We like to point to growth and success. On the other hand, we are haunted by the feeling that the questions are wrong from the start. For a minister to pursue success goals in a business atmosphere may be a breathless climb toward death, all the more damning because the pursuit requires a lifetime of deception. And, following death, the eulogy would be on target: "Poor Rev. Loman, he didn't know who he was."

The dilemma we face is this. How can we answer the question of identity when so many false answers beckon us and when so many good answers seem outdated or inadequate? To call us "the Preacher" seems outdated. To say "the Administrator" or "the Counselor" does not go deep enough. To call us "the Salesperson" is either beguiling or facetious. What other answers exist? Where is the tree of life for the minister, that cosmic center which branches out into the many functions we perform? What is the spring that nourishes our existence, flowing underground beneath the multitude of ministerial duties?

While pondering this problem I was struck by an experience that awakened me to the centrality of religious imagination. Imagination is that creative activity which constantly goes on whether the minister is working on a sermon or a problem of counseling. Out of the abyss, *ex nihilo*, ideas, images, plans, directions seem to flow. Primordial matter is shaped, nonbeing comes forth as being, the void takes on a distinct character for the benefit of others. At the heart of all ministerial functions is creativity. The minister is a seer, a visionary, a dreamer, a planner. The new creation happens. Deep within, some power to create broods over the waters. It will not rest until something comes forth that is new. To sense that power, even to cultivate it, and then to exercise it is the glory of the ministry. In the creative act, which begins in imagination and ends in something produced, we are most like God. The tie to the Creator, the knowledge of the *imago Dei*, is most felt when we exist in some blurred beginning, and are able to say in the darkness, "Let there be light." At that point, Luther's words come true again, "Ye men are gods" (cf. Ps. 82:6; John 10:35), and the question of identity is answered.

Looking back over my ministry, which includes every member canvasses, building fund drives, evangelistic campaigns, preaching missions, and all the housekeeping chores of a local church, I find that the joy in each one is always in proportion to the insight that occurs. For me, the highest joy is still the sermon. This is where creation of image and idea, analysis and exhortation, as well as the art of delivery, give the most "kick." The Scriptures, alongside a pencil and pad, are my paints and canvas, stage and script. The process of seeing the truth of a particular segment of life in relation to the Scriptures carries its own reward for me, quite apart from new members or higher budgets. To answer the question of identity, I am choosing the word "seer" and relating it to that much-debased word "preacher."

Stephen Spender, in a fascinating look at his own vocation as poet, speaks of its mystique. He admits that he has no real worth or "product" except to struggle to clarify. Some truth inside compels him. It struggles and kicks inside until it is born. The birth, if it happens, is now in evidence for others to see and evaluate. Even a harsh evaluation does not stop it, nor does a favorable evaluation propel it. The creative idea exists for expression as fire exists for burning. In a prose poem in his notebook, Spender expresses himself this way:

Bring me peace, bring me power, bring me assurance. Let me reach the bright day, the high chair, the plain desk, where my hand at last controls the words, where anxiety no longer undermines me. If I don't reach there I'm thrown to the wolves, I'm a restless animal wandering from place to place, from experience to experience.

Give me the humility and the judgment to live alone with the deep and rich satisfaction of my own creating: not to be thrown into doubt by a word of spite or disapproval. In the last analysis, don't mind whether your work is good or bad, so long as it has the completeness, the enormity of the whole world which you love.[1]

When ministers feel this way about their work as preachers, or about their work under any other functional label, the question of identity is settled.

This conclusion is the final chapter. To reach it, I must pause beside an experience that was forceful and determinative. From one point of view it was just the intrusion of a new idea, as common as grass. No different from the myriad new ideas that come to everyone. Yet this experience started a train of thought on the subject of religious imagination. It led me down some theological trails, and finally to a vantage point from which to see my ministry in a new light. The trails were interesting in and of themselves. However, the vantage point was more satisfying, since it led to some resolution of the identity problem that was plaguing me into middle age. Who am I? I began to tell myself that I am a seer, with God-given and Godlike powers. Just as Descartes sat before the fire and found the key to his philosophy in "I think, therefore I am," I began to sit before a common creative experience until the phrase "I create, therefore I am" assumed central importance. However, since getting to that conclusion is also important, let me sketch the main road to be traveled, and a few of the side trips.

In Chapter 1, the experience just referred to will be described and critically examined. A creative surge occurred which brought up the subject of religious imagination. The power of the surge and the importance of the subject in relation to sermonizing were undeniable. It was as if a detective were handed a valuable clue after months of fruitless leads. Or, it was as if Archimedes once again cried "Eureka!" from his bathtub. I knew that in an instant I was brought to life with mind at the ready. I was no longer at sea in the vast area of all possibilities. Could it be that the essence, not only of sermons but of the minister's entire life, is tied by a stout cord to that same theme of religious imagination? This is the thesis I will develop.

However, the word "imagination" has a poor press. It appears to be more the stuff of dreams than the bedrock of ministry. What is imagination in general, and religious imagination in particular? This will also be discussed in Chapter 1, and will lead to the following conclusion: that while all imagination is life-giving, religious imagination is unique in at least two ways. Religious imagination proceeds from a mystic center, and it is channeled through the Biblical revelation. The minister consciously studies and ponders that Biblical tradition, and expresses insight in language and thought that has continuity with the ancient story. That tradition and the God behind it are the source of light. Scripture becomes a "glass of vision." The act of seeing and expressing carries the power of life. That is why every sermon is life-giving to the minister whether or not it completes its life-giving connection in the hearer.

This line of thought immediately raises a question for speculation if not for factual knowledge. What is the role of imagination in general as it operates in every province of civilization? Could it be that the use of imagination is a means of grace in all areas of life? Could it also mean that the myriad products of such imagination—evidenced in business and industry, government and community agency, culture and education, worldwide programs and household plans—are all the driving force of divine purpose? Could imagination be the motor for movement toward that far-off great divine event? We will present this possibility and rest the speculative but affirmative answer on deductions both from the doctrine of creation and the broad scheme outlined in Ephesians. Whether the human creation happens to be a song or a sermon, if we are thinking about the internal thrill of being a creative person, there is no special "plus" given to religious imagination that is not given to those in the entire spectrum of creativity. A minister probing a sermonic insight; Archimedes crying "Eureka!"; Alexander Graham Bell exclaiming "What hath God wrought"; even two teen-agers working out a dance routine—all express a power that is resident in the Godhead and imprinted on the race. The power is life-giving, shot through with grace, and useful in the general scheme of things. Man in general, not just religious man or genius or artist, is *homo creator,* just as God the Father of us all is creator in a unique sense. God is "maker of heaven and earth" and we are "makers" too. This broad discussion of creativity, linking religious insight to that of creative people in all fields and linking both to God's creating power will be the theme of Chapter 2.

The purpose of Chapter 2, establishing a connection between all creative people, is to lay some foundation for detecting and profiting by similarities in the creative process. If preachers are linked to all creative people— from artists to computer designers to landscape gardeners to chefs to lawyers—then they might learn from each other, not just in factual knowledge, but in method of operation. However, this discussion must wait until Chapter 4. There is one other group that relied on religious imagination, a group more closely akin to the preacher than the wide gamut of creative people. This group is the great company of apostles and prophets who worked within the time frame of the canon. They were creators, too. Originally, they were called seers. The term "seer" captured the idea of insight and creative grasp. Whatever the phrase "burden of the Lord" meant, or a similar expression, "the hand of the Lord was upon me," it must have described an experience similar to that of a modern preacher who bounces out of bed, grabs a pencil and paper, and jots down an insight before it evaporates. The ancient experience, a response to the question, "Amos, what do you see?" parallels the modern experience of the minister who is also compelled to be a seer. The Biblical preacher and the preacher at First and Madison are united by the power to create, if not by the inner ties of the message itself. The similarity of the two preacher-creators, separated by the centuries, will be the subject of Chapter 3.

To make this comparison is to open up a discussion of many modern theological issues. For instance, a review of the doctrine of inspiration must be attempted. If we maintain the thesis that modern preachers and canonical preachers are of the same family, *homo creator,* with no qualitative difference between them, there is no basis for continuing to use the doctrine of inspiration to mark off Biblical sermons from modern sermons. In recent decades, many scholars have set Scripture apart and elevated it above other writings by the doctrine of inspiration. Bible preachers, so this teaching holds, had an inspiration that is impossible for us today. They had a unique message, whereas we do not. This theory, if true, would damage our thesis, since inspiration is so necessarily tied to creativity. However, the most recent scholarship has noted that this use of the doctrine of inspiration, to mark off canonical Scriptures from noncanonical, is not valid. A study of the early church, for instance, reveals that whereas they believed that the canonical Scriptures were inspired by God, they also believed that postcanonical writings were inspired too. It is as though the inspired interpretation of Biblical events kept spiraling past the book of Revelation so that further light and inspiration would continue to flow.

A second problem is somewhat related to the first.

What is a valid use of imagination as over against a wild and erratic flight of imagination? That is, how can one separate true from false prophets? If the Biblical prophets are akin to modern prophets, how can the former be used to evaluate the latter, without making the latter mere copiers rather than innovators? This problem of separating true from false prophets is a special problem, but it is not peculiar to the twentieth century. It is a problem within the canon as well as in our own times. For instance, Ezekiel's message was often one of judgment. Yet if Ezekiel's message of judgment is turned into a measuring rod for what good prophecy in that period should be, then the message of his contemporary, Isaiah, with its consistent theme of grace, simply would not measure up. Just so, it is not easy to say who speaks for God in any generation. However, this in itself leaves room for the creative interplay of all who preach. Nothing is fully programmed in advance, whether in the sixth century B.C. or in the twentieth century A.D. The spokesperson is overtaken by a "burden," he or she "sees," using all available creative power, and then that person speaks a word that is a new sounding of the Word of God. But it is always open to debate, doubt, and dialogue. The measuring rod is not calibrated with enough accuracy to be absolutely sure.

Therefore, with some risk, but also with exhilaration, the minister as preacher exercises the gift of imagination. He or she moves through a lifetime probing the hidden connections in a constantly moving scene. What is seen, their life and times against the Biblical background of God's ancient activities and eternal purposes, is vital for those who believe that human beings shall not live exclusively in a three-dimensional world. Preachers see the deeper dimension and they proclaim it on behalf of others whose creativity is more developed in other areas, but who nonetheless need the vision so as to live. If preachers achieve nothing else in a lifetime than the capacity to see, that is enough. By this gift they are linked to those in the Bible who exercised the same gift, and also to all creative people who receive their inspiration in areas other than the religious. This discussion—of the link between canonical and modern seers, and some of its theological ramifications—will also be the theme of Chapter 3.

Since there is a universal fellowship of all who see, it is fair to assume that a study of the creative process in other fields than the religious might be fruitful for the minister. If religious imagination has kinship with all imagination, if that is the starting point for all who produce the rich diversity of civilization, then to study what takes place in the creative process may lead to hints that are as valuable to a minister as to a poet or a research scientist. How does the "message" come? Is it always "out of the blue," or is there a place for plodders? Can the message be encouraged? What help is possible to nurture it along? What part do idiosyncrasies play? Does the arrangement of time and schedule make a difference? Is it possible to be creative on schedule fifty-two times a year? These are some of the questions we will encounter in Chapter 4.

The concluding chapter returns to the problem of the minister's identity, and shows how the affirmation "I create, therefore I am" is one important way of providing an answer. Somewhere, deep within, in a mysterious abyss within every person, the Spirit broods over the waters and something new is born. To be ready for that happening, to expect it on a regular basis, is the joy of preaching, as it is the joy of all people involved in the creative process. We do not make a fetish of preaching, nor insist, as in old days, that it is the most important event of the week. For some it is, for many it may not be. Yet the problem today is not so much in overplaying the place of the sermon as it is in relegating the sermon to the back room. We would like to bring it into the front room and introduce it again to any who may have forgotten it was there. The sermon is that creative event which gives life to the seer as well as to those who see through his or her eyes.

From the human point of view, the preacher's creative impact joins with creative impacts in all fields of endeavor, so as to move forward all provinces of civilization. The world lives by the creative power in each of us. That power is the mark of God, stamped indelibly on the human race and waiting to be expressed for the good of all. We who are the creators endure and keep on the growing edge by the continual exercise of the power that flows through us. However frustrating preaching is to a Jeremiah type, the frustration is part of being human, of seeing through a glass darkly, and of seeing for people who comprehend darkly or not at all. Yet, to stifle the hard-to-grasp vision is to die even while continuing to go through the motions of life. Therefore, let us celebrate our originality, together with the great company of preachers of all generations, and continue to look for and expect the burden of the Lord.

On this note the book concludes.

And now, a word on how the book can be used. It is hoped that the largest group of readers will be fellow preachers, many of whom mount the pulpit week by week while wondering what they are doing there. This book might help them to make the passage to greater self-worth. They might see themselves in a mirror and find that the reflected image is not so bad. The book can also be used by ministers who meet in groups to swap notes, share problems, read papers, eat lunch. Certainly some of the material in the book will prompt ministerial discussion, even if it is to disagree. Another group of readers will be those interested in the study of creativity, about which there has been a large body of literature in recent years. This group can include laypeople in all walks of life who are creative themselves and who like to look in on other professions when the source of ideas is up for discussion. It should be obvious that the author sees ministry as no walled-off occupation bathed in a special religious aura. It is hoped that all readers, whether ministers or laypeople, might celebrate the gift we have been given, and be lured into an act of praise, if not into a deeper worship of God. After all, it is a cause for reverence when our minds flutter to life and we say, almost in amazement, Imagine that!

Chapter 1

IMAGINATION: THE LIVELY HEART OF PREACHING

Running up the steps to a dormitory room, hurrying to unpack and get to dinner, I was struck with a creative idea. Without any warning or previous solicitation, the theme of religious imagination marched in and demanded attention. The time was most inauspicious. The place was a steaming hot room on the fourth floor, and there was pressure to unpack and get to dinner. The intruder took no account of these pedestrian things. The theme suggested the possibility for exploration, at least an essay, perhaps a book. How did it get through the other anxieties I felt? Why did it select that particular moment? I had not been reading on the subject of creativity or imagination. No one had mentioned the phrase to me. Yet here it was, a vague central idea and a dim awareness that a group of topics might cluster around it.

"Out of the Blue!" Or Was It?

I was impressed by the force of the intruder. Once it was locked in, it dominated my action at the two-week summer conference. Whereas I usually attended every lecture, workshop, and special event, the weight of something—was it the "burden of the Lord," or just the "burden"?—drove me to miss these and find the library and the typing room. Why? Where did it all originate? Why was the topic so compelling? It arose like laughter. It drifted in like a mood and then hung around. It is no wonder that the ancients—like many who are not so ancient—felt that inspiration and the suddenness of it was a visitation from whatever gods there be. As Robert Louis Stevenson said about his own experience as a writer, "The real work is done by some unseen collaborator." And even Nietzsche, no mystic in the ordinary sense, recalls his own burst of inspiration with the comment, "One can hardly reject completely the idea that one is the mere incarnation, or mouthpiece, or medium of some almighty power."[2]

My first impression about this compulsive suggestion for a theme was erroneous. I thought the idea came "out of the blue," as if my mind was a *tabula rasa* until it was invaded by an inspiration. I have come to believe differently. I had experienced the excitement of a new idea that seemed so novel as to have no precedents at all. At least, for the moment, I failed to look for any. Yet I have become convinced that no creative idea comes totally "out of the blue," without preparation. A hiker may be surprised to look down at his black-and-red jacket and find all kinds of traveling seeds and spores, each hooked by the ingenious mechanisms of nature, but the hiker chose first to walk through a field in the fall, and not along a seacoast in the spring.

It took some distance from the summer conference before I realized some of the input behind the event. I had become obsessed with the idea of religious imagination, but that was an end product of a chain of events and ideas. First of all, I had been asked to write a minibook that might be expanded if the circumstances were favorable. Secondly, I had just received a rejection slip from a publisher regarding a series of sermons. "Sermons don't sell," he said. "They must be cast in some other form." Thirdly, I like to write, just as I like to preach. Perhaps "like" is not the right word. Both enterprises are painful, frustrating, and at times impossible. If I could escape them, I would. They remind me of a beagle in our neighborhood who chases cars. He never quite makes it; he probably wouldn't know what to do if he did; yet the chase is more enticing than the exhaustion. Just so, I like to write and preach, and find it an exhausting, exhilarating enterprise. Last of all, at the midpoint in my life, I was haunted with a feeling of emptiness in my profession.

What is my skill? If I were an auto mechanic, I would define my skill in terms of cars repaired and put back on the road. The new models would give me new specific things to learn. If car repairing were my thing, I could go through life with definite skills and growing ability and be satisfied. But what does a minister do whose specialty is preaching? "My, you have a wonderful way with words," one friend told me. But of what value is that? Words in themselves seem like the smile of the Cheshire Cat, an apparition with no substance. At their best, words are from a voice crying in the wilderness; at their worst, they are "sicklied o'er with the pale cast of thought." Sometimes words become substitutes for action. These days, the cry is for action, for needed skills, for abilities that bulldoze the wilderness and build factories and homes. A preacher's skill, a gift of using words, seemed unwarranted and unneeded. Lewis Carroll had said it:

> Beware the Jabberwock, my son!
> . . . .
> The Jabberwock, with eyes of flame

Came whiffling through the tulgey wood
And burbled as it came!

This latter unease was the dark side of my mind when
I ran up the stairs at the summer conference. A possible
threat to my professional existence. Twenty ministerial
years, and the one thing I do well seemed to have no more
value than the "cloth" the weavers used for the emperor's
"new clothes." I began my ministry thinking the sermon
was the most important event in the week. Granted, this
is a narrow view of ministry, and fortunately other ministers excel in other areas. But to develop a speaking skill,
to have abilities in that area, and then to find that the
sentences are gossamer threads is devastating. Again,
thinking of the emperor's clothes, I felt that I was walking
down the street when some little child on the sidelines
spoke truthfully and said, "Look, the Emperor is naked."
A publisher had rejected a sheaf of sermon manuscripts.
All that was left was for young people in the congregation
to get up during the sermon and walk out tittering,
"Nothing in that for me."

Then, "Pow!" It struck. Seemingly from nowhere, actually from a series of immediate tensions and question-
ings. What is it you do? I had raised the question as if it
had no important answer. That day the answer came, and
it was important. It gave significance to the years when
I stressed the sermon and gave it a priority of my time.
You are a person who exercises insight, who struggles to
see. Religious imagination! That is the background of
every sermon. Without it, the lights would go out above
the pulpit. I remembered that the early term for the
prophet was "seer." In early days, these seers looked at
prosaic two-plus-two's, and saw enormous amounts. The
plus was the eternal dimension. They found hidden con-

nections between the tradition and their times, and the lines went back into God, and forward into some kingdom to come. They were seers who used those frail things called words, whereby they transported ideas and conveyed directions. That is the tradition in which I stand.

"Come, be a seer" is another way of interpreting my original call to the ministry. From this, my mind jumped to a passage in the New Testament that is usually misinterpreted: "Eye hath not seen, . . . nor ear heard, . . . the things which God hath prepared for those who love him. But God hath revealed them unto us by his Spirit." (I Cor. 2:9.) The misinterpretation makes this passage speak of heaven and what we will see someday when we have full vision. Nothing of the kind! Paul is speaking of the here and now, and of possibilities that exist under the leading of the Spirit. The underside of life, or the high reaches of the ordinary, these can be seen by the Spirit within us. God is revealing them. Seers are needed.

Again, the meaning dawned of the importance of religious imagination, important enough for a vocation. Here is a foundational meaning for any minister who feels that preaching is his or her special skill. We are linked with all those who from distant times have tried to see the inner connections of things and relate these to divine purpose. We are possessed by the apocalyptic hope that a clear day will come when we can see forever, even while we know realistically that insights come more like manna, with just enough for one weary day and a few miles of a long journey.

The original impulse, religious imagination, played tricks. It exploded in all directions like fireworks. It lured like a Siren. It was sweet-sounding and threatening. Above all, it was life-giving. It is always life-giving to find creative ideas racing through your mind, suggesting new goals and directions. This is particularly true when, in middle age, the dullness of the routine settles in, plus the vague hint that the tide of life might be flowing out to sea. But the threat is also there: hours and months to read, write and rewrite, discard; to pursue ideas, many of which end up at a blank wall; to experience the uneasy feeling that what is important for you might mean nothing to someone else; or that what is vital as an initial impulse can't be developed beyond the impulse. It is no wonder that Hector Berlioz once woke up with a dream for a composition but, remembering the tortuous road in writing other compositions, simply turned his back on it until the inspiration died.

Imagination versus Creativity

Obviously, there is a vast difference between an inspiration and the finished product of paragraphs, chapters, and coherent ideas. My theme introduced itself as religious imagination, but imagination is the inner work of a flash impulse. The gift of imagination, or inspiration, is vastly different from the completion of a book, painting, or musical composition. The latter mean that the original idea has pushed through to a conclusion, available to others. The pushing through is the hard part, since resistance comes from everything, from laws of grammar to the need for a marketable unity. The pen against the paper may be too sluggish for the racing of the mind. Even barking dogs, phone bells, and train whistles are part of the labyrinth of obstacles that an original idea must traverse before it is born into the real world. Let the term "creation" stand for the finished product, and the word "imagination" be left for the original impulse. An artist struggles to create out of the available impulse of the imagination. Only in rare cases is the struggle avoided.

The distinction between imagination and creation, both separated by an intervening struggle, is helpful. It explains the weekly experience of the preaching minister, who receives imaginative power in small doses, and who will be just as caught up in an idea as I was when bounding up the steps to my dormitory. In either case, imagination waits to be turned into a creation. The difference is only in degree, not in kind. In sermonizing, the creation out of imagination must come on a weekly schedule. In essays and books, the gestation period is longer. For both, there is the struggle, tension, fear, and often late-Saturday toil.

Rollo May cites the case of a young man under his care who kept coming up with ideas for a novel, but got his kicks in imagination only. Once he pictured a general direction for the plot, and felt that he had the makings of a novel, he promptly went on to other things.[3] That is the extreme of imagination without creation. Some others—notably inventors, though not necessarily these —often get the completed tangible idea along with the original imaginative thrust. This is a case, relatively rare, of imagination leading to creation without the intervening struggle, fear, and exodus. The composer Mozart exemplifies this:

When I am, as it were, completely myself, entirely alone . . . , say travelling in a carriage, or walking after a good meal, or during the night when I cannot sleep; it is on such occasions that my ideas flow best and most abundantly. . . . Those pleasures that please me, I retain in my memory, and am accustomed, as I have been told, to hum them to myself. If I continue in this way, it soon occurs to me how I may turn this or that morsel to account . . . agreeably to the rules of counterpoint, to the peculiarities of the various instruments, etc. All this fires my soul, and provided I am not disturbed, my subject enlarges itself, becomes methodized and defined, and the whole, though it be long, stands almost complete and finished in my mind so that I can survey it, like a fine picture or a beautiful statue, at a glance. . . . For this reason, the committing to paper is done quickly enough, for everything is, as I have said before, already finished.[4]

The Mozart method is wonderful and may even be the popular image most have of the creative process. According to this method, the impulse comes; the full dimension of the finished piece is given; the struggle is eliminated. The wind of the creative spirit blows steady and straight. All that remains is the transcription. The analogy between this caricature of the creative process and certain stories of verbal inspiration can easily be detected. Scripture writers, so the theory goes, received their vision and directions with startling clarity and minimum effort. They were told what to write. The word of the Lord *came;* the Lord *spoke;* they were given a dream, a vision, a few stone tablets already transcribed. They were receivers and hence passive. God was the active source of the inspiration.

If this is the way Mozart and Moses did their work, and this is made normative for the creative process, then the uniqueness of Scripture writers is guaranteed. The distance between us and them is a vast gulf permanently fixed. The theory is attractive for those who wish to show *a priori* that Scripture writers are in a class all by themselves. However, the Mozart experience is rare. Most creative people testify to hard work, with partial insights, plus the struggle to produce. The struggle threatens to block the imagination. Where it is wrestled with, fought through to the other side, a creation occurs. And, surprisingly, the pain of the struggle is often imprinted on the creativity, and gives it enduring worth.

The same might be said of Scripture writers too. For every one who seems to hear an audible voice or sharply delineated dream, even taking those descriptions at face value, many other Biblical speakers feel otherwise. They are baffled spirits trying to lay hold of an inspiration that constantly eludes them. "O that I knew where I might find him," says Job (ch. 23:3). Again he says, "I go forward, and he is not there; and backward, but I cannot perceive him" (ch. 23:8). "My God, why . . . ?" cries a psalmist (Ps. 22:1). "We see through a glass, darkly," Paul testifies (I Cor. 13:12). There is more of a kinship between most creative people in and out of Scripture who struggle with their creations than there is with those who radiate an aura of effortless genius. For most, the originating idea is a vague awareness of something important. Let the word "imagination" stand for that starting point. The ensuing creation, the actual bringing forth of something new, is a painstaking effort. When the imagination has triggered the effort to produce something available to others, the finished work can be described by the word "creation."

The poet A. E. Housman probably speaks for more creative people than Mozart in indicating the balance between flashes of insight, usually intermittent, and the hard work of craftsmanship:

Having drunk a pint of beer at luncheon . . . I would go out for a walk of two or three hours. As I went along, thinking of nothing in particular . . . , there would flow into my mind with sudden and unaccountable emotion, sometimes a line or two of a verse, sometimes a whole stanza at once, accompanied, not preceded, by a vague notion of the poem which they were destined to form part of. . . . When I got home I wrote them down, leaving gaps and hoping that further inspiration might be forthcoming another day. Sometimes it was . . . but sometimes the poem had to be taken in hand and completed by the brain, which was apt to be a matter of trouble and anxiety, involving trial and disappointment and sometimes ending in failure.[5]

This description is closer to most published descriptions of the creative process. There are flashes of insight, a few of which slide ready-made into place, plus hints that are hard to pick up and that require struggle. It seems that the muse captures the interest before setting her followers in the middle of a rocky road. Housman describes one stanza of a poem that would not come by any coaxing of the imagination. He says that he wrote it thirteen times and it was more than a "twelvemonth" before he got it right.[6]

There are other ways of looking at the connection between imagination and the end product of creation, the first so free and insightful, the latter so difficult; the first an instantaneous invasion, the second thirteen tries over a twelvemonth. The imagination seems to fly above the intellect, doing rolls and dives in an instant of time. The imagination is akin to the mystical experience, where years of toil get condensed into a moment of time. The mystical, unhindered for the moment by logic and motivated by a force outside the will, touches reality. A wing of an angel seems to beat, where rules of grammar or sentence structure do not inhibit. This area of brooding or meditation has none of the encumbrances of logic or of unified development. The mind is like an empty night sky into which the rocket of an idea explodes, dazzling. Thomas Aquinas, after writing his massive *Summa,* had such a mystical experience in Naples. He commented that this experience meant more than all he had written previously. Usually the order is reversed: first the insight, then the *Summa.*

The *Summa,* the working out of the imagination so that it can join the creation, is the hard part. The angels have withdrawn. The ideas must become incarnate in grammar and sentences. Orderly sequence and discursive development must give shape to the intuition, and this for two reasons. First of all, the one who is given the ethereal, weightless burst needs to think it through discursively to see what it is that has laid hold on him or her. Arthur Koestler, for instance, who disclaims any intuitions of a mystical sort, feels he is led on day by day in his writing to see for himself what ending his story will have. He begins with a vague gestalt, and not with a ready-made story.[7] So, first of all, the creation must follow the imaging to understand just what was in the sealed orders. But further, the creation must happen if others are to share the impulse of the author, and be able to see what the author sees. The drive from imagination to creation is slow and frustrating. Were it not that every insight or imaginative burst carries with it the inherent demand to be expressed, the creation may never happen, at least by those who do not have the rare Mozart gift of seeing things complete from the beginning.

Rollo May recounts the struggle of a famous portrait painter, Alberto Giacometti, in painting a portrait of his friend, James Lord.[8] The latter came to the studio and sat in the prescribed pose. Then he noted certain things about his painter friend. First of all, the extreme anxiety of the artist was evident in delaying tactics. Giacometti would often disconsolately occupy himself for half an hour or more doing odds and ends, literally afraid to begin. And the basis of the fear? Lord correctly assumed that the anxiety was related to the gap between the ideal vision that the artist was trying to paint and the objective results. He discussed this contradiction, which every artist experiences:

This fundamental contradiction arising from the hopeless discrepancy between conception and realization is at the root of all artistic creation, and it helps explain the anguish which seems to be an unavoidable component of that experience. Even as "happy" an artist as Renoir was not immune to it.

What meant something, what alone existed with a life of its own was his [Giacometti's] indefatigable, interminable struggle via the act of painting to express in visual terms a perception of reality that had happened to coincide momentarily with my head [which Giacometti was then trying to paint]. To achieve this was of course impossible, because what is essentially abstract can never be made concrete without altering its essence. But he was committed, he was in fact condemned to the attempt, which at times seemed rather like the task of Sisyphus.[9]

From inspired imagination to creative production is a heaven to earth movement, an incarnation. Intruding ideas, which dazzle with possibilities, must get caught in the sticky web of logic and grammar, the limits of the creator and the audience, the confinement of time and material—thirteen tries in a twelvemonth for Housman; indefatigable, interminable struggle for Giacometti.

"Plodding" is the term to describe most creations. Creators inch along from the first inspiration until their road makes a partial stop in a creation. This is my experience in sermonizing. It was to be the same when the theme "religious imagination" broke the lock of my mind and took over the place. I stood off and observed the happening. Certain attitudes and feelings grouped around the theme. I wanted to be alone. It was almost like crawling into some creative center to give birth to something you hope will not be stillborn. And please note—the desire for birth is both of the finished product, the essay or book, and of myself, the creator. Just as the product was being shaped, and the final appearance determined by little bits, so the feeling was born deep inside that I was coming alive too. My mind was kicking against its confinements. Either book and author would be born alive, or both would be stillborn. This is not a healthy state of mind, yet it is not an uncommon one. Again, quoting May on the painter Giacometti, the latter is "obliged to feel that it is necessary to start his entire career over again every day, as it were, from scratch."[10] One should not be so tied to one's job or work that one suffers or rejoices symbiotically with its failures or successes. Yet I am trying to observe the process rather than evaluate it. An incremental advance toward life or death was involved. Perhaps this explains the mixture of anguish and ecstasy that was present—anguish, because you never know if you have enough energy to bring to focus the vague idea; ecstasy, because you are immediately pulled from boredom to aliveness. For the moment, nothing else matters. The cold, measured distance between subject and object disintegrates. You stand outside yourself and into something, where distinctions of this and that, I and it, have disappeared. Even God is not an object up there, or outside. The meaning of God is also fused into the creative process. As musicians in the act of improvising do not think of distinct notes, but just flow with it; or as lovers in the act of making love merge with each other and the world as well; just so, the creator in the act of catching an inspiration knows the ecstasy of fusion. It is almost as if the Genesis story is repeated: God breathed into man, and man became a living being.

Imagination, Creativity, and the Preacher

I thought back over my preaching ministry and tried to relate what I felt in that weekly or twice-weekly production, the sermon. Actually the similarities were remarkable. In every case, religious imagination was involved, whether the sermon flowed out easily or had to be fought through. Once the ideas locked into each other and had the ring of authenticity, at that moment I felt that I too was coming alive. The fact that the topic of religious imagination promised a longer struggle than the weekly sermon did not diminish the importance of the sermon as a life-giving bit of weekly excitement. Could it be that for ministers who have preaching as their focus, the working through of weekly inspiration keeps them always a few feet above boredom through the years? To see the connections between the times of the Bible and today; to stand at that point between God's acts then and now; to feel the tug between the mundane and the supramundane and to work this through to a proclamation is the little "Aha!" of discovery that we are always privileged to make.

What happens in sermonizing? The text grabs your imagination in a vague way. You work to make the vagueness explicit. You sit before a blank sheet of paper and let the text call forth ideas, comments, humor, scholarship, personal notes, anything that may or may not be helpful. The imagination proceeds to unify the material around a theme, and prompts you to throw out 90 percent of the mental ramblings you have set down. The final product, the sermon, has as much imaginative thrust as you can include. It represents the total insides of you at that particular moment. It is not like a term paper, which is assigned from the outside to meet a requirement. Term paper topics are usually another's selection of what is vital. The sermon is much more personal. The topic for the sermon is what you have selected, or perhaps what has selected you. It involves openness to God, text, personality, and all the input of the human situation. Always there is the throb of life about it. Every sermon should be at least a nine-hour birth process of something that is bone of your bone and flesh of your flesh. By it, both you and the topic come alive. For me, a sermon is being grabbed somewhere in the imagination by a text, being excited by the subject, and laboring to present the truth of that text imaginatively so that others can be grabbed by it too.

One mark, then, of the imagination is excitement. This is true whether for book or sermon. Productions that lack this beginning may throw a lot of words and dogma over the valley floor, but none will come together with the breath of life and dance around. Nor do these lackluster productions move the hearers. Nothing said from the pulpit becomes fresh for you or for others until it has passed through the caldron of your imagination and come up glowing with enthusiasm. Here the staleness is burned away and something authentic is refined.

Imagination brings together intellect, emotion, and will in a constellation surrounded by a thousand subterranean forces. By conscious openness to these forces, and by the refusal to proceed until the nudge comes, you become an authentic person, a better preacher, a theologian who can escape the dust of dry phrases. In other words, you become a communicator of the faith who has a following beyond the theological guild. For instance, Robert Frost might have crafted lines on the need to get on with the duties of life and not become entranced too long by its mysteries. He could have hacked out some such lines at any time. But one particular night, so he tells a friend of E. W. Sinnott, he opened his front door and strode out into the snowy darkness for a breath of air. In those few moments, there came to his mind the whole of that intriguing poem, "Stopping by Woods on a Snowy Evening."[11] That is the nudge, the excitement, the commanding intuition, the summons to write or preach.

I had an inkling of the importance of my original theme, religious imagination. It hinted that the term "seer" contained the essence of the minister's identity. In the act of seeing, we who preach are following a distinctive cloud and pillar of fire, and we might be sustained for a lifetime while on a long trek. This would be true whether the church we serve is big or small, urban or rural, or whether the congregation rose to acclaim us or simply rose to recess. By the legitimate use of religious imagination, we preachers would be staying alive.

The expression "staying alive" sounds so selfish. We have been taught to give our life away, to be self-abnegating, altruistic, always for others. Up to a point, this is true. Yet, paradoxically, if we have no real sense of being alive, what do we have to give? Life must pulse inside before it has any meaning for others. The woebegone, down-in-the-mouth image that many ministers portray in their function as preacher is hardly a gift to be placed on anyone's altar. That is why, at the risk of sounding selfish, we preachers must lay claim to a legitimate self-centeredness. We must ask what there is in what we do that really makes us come alive. This must be asked first, rather than the more usual question, What can we do to make others come alive? The first question may answer the second, but the second can never be answered without coming to terms with the first. For this reason, Timothy is instructed to pay attention to his spiritual endowments, those which are involved in preaching and teaching, because, by doing so, he will save himself as well as his hearers (I Tim. 4:16).

The counsel to save ourselves makes us squirm. It sounds unchristian. Yet it is essential for any joyous self-giving. When Jesus said, "Because I live, you will live also" (John 14:19), he was assuming that it was good to be alive. Preachers must begin there, too, by affirming that they are alive in the vocation to which they have been called. They are called to see, to exercise a religious imagination on behalf of those who sit in darkness. It is not wrong to find delight in the process, and be sustained by it, whether or not tangible results appear in the lives of others.

If it is true that imagination is the lively heart of preaching, we should appreciate it more. Imagination is a powerful gift with a powerfully poor press. It is the Cinderella who stays home while the other sisters prepare for the ball. Why is this so, when the sisters are really quite ugly? The reasons are many. We think of the imagined as nebulous, almost unreal. A sermon we can read and evaluate. The same is true of a book. But the impulse that prompted these is out of sight, ethereal, a will-o'-the-wisp. We even have ways of disparaging what we cannot understand. "He's only imagining things," we say. "It's all in her imagination." "He's a victim of a vivid imagination." The word sounds vague, illusory, divorced from real life. When we say of something we have heard, "Imagine that!" the implication is that this something is hard to believe. Even when we speak more positively, the word is on the verge of being turned into a pumpkin. Thus, we may say of a book that it is an imaginative piece. We mean to compliment it; however, there is still the implication of escapism rather than realism; of the graceful and beautiful rather than the forceful. To all these attempts at downgrading imagination, we must call a halt. That which is being disparaged is the mysterious life of all we do as preachers. By the weekly use of imagination, the Spirit bears witness with our spirit that we have God-given credentials. We are seers.

But then, so are painters, teachers, social workers, lawmakers, chefs, and carpenters. They are seers too. Imagination is not just the headwaters for a book or a sermon. It is also the mysterious source of creativity in all parts of civilization. It is in imagination that all beginning ideas start to flow, whether they end up in sermons or in paintings, in mathematical discoveries, new recipes, or new do-it-yourself ideas. All creativity involves a seeing. All creativity involves a power or energy that drives the would-be creator to express the hidden thing. All creativity probably gives as its special gift the touch of life.

Marks of Religious Imagination

This fact, the universality of seeing, raises a special problem. How is religious imagination different from imagination in general? If all imagination is a vision of a possibility, if all imagination sees unusual connections, if all imagination propels toward a creation, what is so unique about religious imagination? What are its distinctives? What sets the minister off from the artist, the statesman, the chef, the poet? Basically just two things: minister-seers rely on a transcendent source, and minister-seers make Scripture a glass of vision. Let's examine these two.

Nowhere is the creative person more aware of the divine source than in the ministry. The minister is a person of God. Apologies or vague musings aside, he or she knows that ideas don't just come out of the blue. They come from a divine Somewhere. Therefore, the minister is one who prays for insight from God, and is as open to it from that source as is a person who seeks a certain kind of music by switching from AM to FM. The station is already identified. Its call letters are recognized. The reception is received with joy even when covered with interference. Emil Brunner used to say that reading Scripture was like listening to old RCA records, played before solid state and the Dolby System. There was a lot of needle noise and static; nevertheless, if one listened closely, the message came through. One heard "his master's voice."

We will not deny that every act of inspiration could be a divine prompting. The master's voice comes in many strange accents. In fact, it would be odd if all God's speaking was in Biblical language and totally within the church-made rubric of salvation history. There is some primal center within each of us, Christian or not. We draw on this for our basic life-style, our values, our dominant faith, and for that well of creative energy which drives the inventive genius of civilization. However, ministers above all others are certain that this source is connected with God and his Son, Jesus Christ. It is a matter of conscious faith for ministers that in God we live and move and have our being.

The wind of the Spirit is the creativity that blows through our minds. Without this, it would be academic to speak of a new thing that God is doing. Without this, we might as well head for the desert and be disillusioned, Elijah-style. But no. The new keeps coming. In the Spirit, according to Paul—and with a great deal of wonder—we actually have the mind of Christ. What no eye has seen, even the eye that may be wonderfully creative in other areas, God has revealed to us by his Spirit (I Cor. 2:9, 10, 16). Therefore, though the upsurge of insight may be from the subconscious, or from an unusual set of circumstances, or from a chance line in a book, or from the newspaper, God is speaking. After all, if Nietzsche felt that he could hardly reject the idea that he was the mouthpiece of some almighty power, the Christian minister should not be embarrassed by confessing this. Just as prophets received some word from God from outside themselves, so the minister listens. He or she allows what is heard to become a "burden." The struggle begins; one works through ideas, language, distraction, schedule. The Spirit again broods over the waters. The light of the first day for that particular message dawns. It is good. An aspect of the mind of Christ is felt, which was shaped into a sermonic word.

Ministry through preaching begins and continues through encounter with Christ. At that point, seeing of another dimension begins. Look at the birds, said Jesus, and hang up your anxieties. Consider the lilies, and remember that you too will be clothed. Ponder the falling sparrow, and remember that you are not a number to God. Look at the fields ready for harvest, if you should ever think your world looks like a burnt-over district. When Jesus gathered disciples he gave them the power to see things they otherwise would pass by. It was a poet's eye that saw an even deeper dimension than beauty.

Needless to say, though the minister is drawing from the same divine source, the mind of Christ, it is not a static Christ. That is, what touches the imagination is not some bathrobed figure, nor a word that dances through the mind and comes out in old English. Rather, it is a Christ who is on the road, whose face is semihidden or lucid for moments, and who is always going before us into some Galilee. Now he appears on some beach shrouded in morning mist; later he disappears, only to reappear on some unused road. But, strangely, wherever he appears, he is relating to those who are troubled about problems of the day—the poor, the poor in spirit, the sick, the emotionally sick, the bedeviled, and the walked over. Something of Christ meets something of contemporary times and the spark of meaning is struck, particularly involving the dispossessed.

The important thing for ministry through preaching is not to be simply a creative person, but to be conscious of a creativity coming from a divine source. Malcolm Muggeridge, the former editor of *Punch* and an incisive commentator on the modern scene, gave his own description of an experience of transcendence. It happened in Bethlehem. Literally. He was doing a show for the BBC at Christmastime. Shots were made of the town, the surrounding fields, and the inside of the Church of the Nativity. Peddlers mixed with pilgrims, crass commercialism mixed with piety. One shepherd, sensing an opportunity, picked up a sheep and held it while the cameraman zoomed in with his lens. Yet it was not a total act of kindness. When the picture-taking ended, the shepherd was ready with palm out and argued when the coins given were deemed insufficient. With a feeling of "Let's get this over with and get out," Muggeridge entered the dark interior of the Church of the Nativity and sat patiently in an alcove until the last pilgrim had passed by. How different the scene was from the days of Christ, he thought. Candles, incense, ornaments, brocades, silver inlay at the spot where the Christ was supposedly born. All this, plus the ever-present beggar and the numerous tourist traps. But then, as Muggeridge studied the faces of the pilgrims, he saw that what looked phony to him was transforming to them. Underneath the encrustation, the spirit of Jesus seemed to bring forth genuine feelings in them of reverence, wonder, calm. They would cross themselves, or bow, or stand a moment and leave. Could it be that hidden underneath this there is something real? In such a way, the train of insight started that led Muggeridge to return to faith and later to write the book *Rediscovering Jesus.*

All conversion experiences participate in the transcendent source, and this often leads to a new kind of seeing:

> The angels keep their ancient places;—
> Turn but a stone and start a wing!
> 'Tis ye, 'tis your estrangèd faces,
> That miss the many-splendoured thing.[12]

The many-splendored thing is everyplace. There seems to be no limit to the seeing. Jesus himself said that he had much to reveal that could not be revealed to the disciples, but that would be revealed later. That indicates a process and fast shuttling between Christ and art, Christ and science, politics and faith, Scripture and newspaper, tradition and experience. Nothing is off limits. Sitting in a dark church alcove, crossing the street at Times Square, walking outside the house on a cold New England night, one finds that signals from the primal source are constantly popping through and commanding attention. Tillich spoke of a "method of correlation," where the world in its complexity raises the questions for which the gospel is intended as the answer. But the correlation is accomplished in its initial stages by an act of seeing.

To see requires a conscious contact with the living God. But it also requires Scripture. Religious imagination makes of Scripture a glass of vision. The living God is not a pool of emotion, so that all the preacher has to do is to jump in once in a while for refreshment. That might describe some forms of mysticism, though in a very flip way. The God infiltrating the minister's imagination is the God of Abraham, Isaac, and Jacob; the God of history who struggles to bring a people out of Egypt, who entered our times and knows our mentality, who loves and gives, suffers and dies. This is the God who calls and re-creates the called, the God who unites us in Christ to do Christ-like things. As soon as any content is given to religious imagination, the record of God's mighty acts must be read. In this book the hints are embedded for new directions, or for a word of judgment, or perhaps of encouragement. In the reading of Scripture—best read, as Barth suggests, with the Bible in one hand and the newspaper in the other—the divine "Aha!" starts clicking in the mind.

Other creative fields do not anchor themselves so. A Biblically oriented mathematician is no better as a mathematician, neither is a Bible-reading chemical engineer more creative in his field than those who never express faith. It is quite the reverse with the minister. Christian ministers as preachers would have little to say if they did not attend to Scripture. The image of Luther casts a long shadow over the Christian pulpit. When Luther uttered his famous protest at the Diet of Worms, he affirmed: "My conscience is bound to the Word of God. Here I stand. I can do no other. God help me. Amen." He was speaking for all ministers whose vocation it is to speak for God.

Scripture is the seedbed of the minister's thought. Here the insight germinates as the minister throws in personal experience, reading, contemporary history, future plans. The hidden assumption in preaching is that a book which spans a little over thirteen hundred years (and those mostly B.C.), as well as five cultures alien to our own, can still be the springboard into the minds of every generation. By this revelation that is printed, revelation continues. Muggeridge may have an experience of divine reality in the crypt of the Church of the Nativity, but even this is unconsciously conditioned by the vast store of Biblical knowledge already in Muggeridge's mind. Scripture is the glass of vision in each era, and often in surprisingly offbeat ways. No other creative discipline anchors itself to one spot in quite the same way, and from this single vantage point claims to see in all directions.

What is it about the Scriptures that give them this power in the creative process? Is it a secret that God has and only the ordained initiates prove? Is it a bit of divine magic, continuing the urim and thummim of the Old Testament? No. These answers are nonsense. The power of the Scriptures is in the power of the story they tell, which in the telling gives continuity with the past and also insight that is fresh. Let me illustrate.

People who share the same story have a bond of identity that those who are outside the story do not possess. One of the fun things about family reunions after years of separation is to trigger the memory by recalling "the time when"—when the children were young, when the birthdays came, when we vacationed on the lake, when we moved back east. The "whens" fly off in all directions and seem so trivial. Yet it is by the repetition of "whens" that family identity is kept and the bonds of unity are strengthened. To an outsider, someone else's storytelling is boring. That person has another story, unless perhaps the story being told can be penetrated. An outsider who marries into the family brings a story and claims the story already told. Immigrants coming into a country likewise bring a story, but they also accept one in the country they enter. They are no longer people without a country, condemned to wander.

Who are we of the church? Obviously, we are people who share the same story. Who are the Jews? People who were called out of Egypt, who were called into covenant, who remember the God of Abraham, Isaac, and Jacob. It is not a coincidence that the refrain of "I am the God who brought you up out of the land of Egypt" is repeated in most books of the Old Testament, and on into the New Testament. The power of a similar story is the bond of identity. Elie Wiesel, modern novelist-theologian, who reflects the pathos felt by the Jewish people after facing recent attempts and threats of genocide, also realizes the power of the story in the life of Judaism when that story is repeated endlessly. In introducing *The Enchanted Forest,* Wiesel quotes an old Chasidic tale of the Baal Shem Tov: The ancient *tsaddik* went to an exact spot in the forest, told the story, lit a fire, and offered prayer, and the miracle happened. In the next generation, the rabbi forgot the spot, but he told the story, lit the fire, and prayed, and the miracle happened. Years passed, and the next rabbi forgot the spot and never lit the fire, but he told the story and prayed, and the miracle happened. Generations later, the rabbi forgot the spot, didn't light the fire and couldn't remember the prayer, but he told the story—and still the miracle happened. That is a Jewish story, but shot through with Christian implications. When Jesus said, "Do this in remembrance of me," he encouraged the generations following to be bound to himself by telling the story.

But stories do not merely hold together the people of God. In telling this story, as in telling all stories, thousands of computer connections take place in the mind that keep printing out new messages. For instance, in the Bicentennial celebrations of 1976 in the United States, Thomas Jefferson came through in some circles as virtually the founder of the NAACP. In telling the story of the Declaration of Independence, it was remembered that the original draft of this famous document had included a paragraph condemning slavery. Apparently, Jefferson felt keenly the plight of an estimated 450,000 blacks in a nation of only three or four million colonists. Talk of freedom for all, and of unalienable rights, was hypocrisy while a large portion of the population remained disinherited. The paragraph had to be deleted back then, but how timely it was in a new '76! The mere remembrance gave impetus to reform. After a Civil War, and a civil rights movement, and a continuing movement toward equality, we Americans wanted to see that the nation had the freedom theme in its origins. Even one of the Founding Fathers, Jefferson, knew the need for freedom for all. Freedom for blacks was the unfinished business of the Revolution. In telling our story in a Bicentennial year, we picked up and emphasized this hidden historical note.

Just so, every story has a forward direction. People tell stories to gain perspective. The Bible in its story of redemption opens up vistas of new redemptions. That is why the minister-as-preacher doesn't wonder or become embarrassed by confessing his reliance upon the Word of God in a way that other creative disciplines do not. Every sermon is a springboard from continuity to some contemporary situation. For example, a white professor who preached recently in a black church in New York City happened to give his own translation of the parable of the rich man and Lazarus. The rich man asked that Lazarus might give him a cup of water to stop his thirst. The next line was translated freely by the professor: "Lazarus ain't gonna be your boy no more." Just that line, but with it, laughter erupted for five minutes. The old story had broken into the imagination with a not-to-be-missed implication.

Not every minister shares the Bible story. Some have explicitly cut themselves off from it. This does not impugn their usefulness to God or to fellow human beings. It does mean that they have stepped over the line from being Christian preachers to another vocation. One conspicuous example of this is Sam Keen. In *To a Dancing God*, Keen reviews his own life story, and his restless search for meaning. Part of the review involves his relation to the Christian tradition. Instead of finding meaning and insight in this, he describes it as part of his problem, something that he needed to throw off before he could really live with himself. He reports on his homecoming, which is a new life without the Scripture tradition.

It may be that homecoming is the secularized or deparochialized equivalent of what Christians traditionally mean by justification by faith. For both Paul and Luther, justification involved the realization that human salvation was not contingent upon any human action. . . . Yet Paul and Luther still do not point a universal way beyond exile, for they made salvation depend upon appropriating an event in the past—the life, death and resurrection of Christ. In order to appropriate this event, the contemporary believer must adopt alien moral, intellectual and philosophical categories from a time in history that is not his own. Justification by faith leaves me in exile from the historical time of my incarnate existence, if it makes belief in the unique atoning work of Christ a condition of salvation.[13]

This approach can be full of insight and hope as a psychology or philosophy. But terms like "God," "justification by faith," "exile and homecoming," and "grace" simply float off from the tradition in which they were moored. They have the form of religion while denying the power of the story behind them.

Minister-preachers do not feel this way. They go to Scripture because that is their home, where windows look out in all directions. When they are home, they are most perceptive. The Bible is then no straitjacket to their minds, any more than Faulkner is narrowed by the South or Frost by the New England countryside. Instead, for all these seers, a cosmopolitan view is spawned in the provincial. For the preacher, a narrow segment of God's activity —the Biblical story—gives the fuller word that God so loved the world. The overtones from cross and resurrection sound in the marketplace. Instead of the Bible causing myopia, it becomes a glass of vision for both preacher and congregation who might otherwise be lost in the maze of common contemporary circumstances.

Thus, two marks of religious imagination exist which set it off from imagination in general: a conscious tie to the divine source and a repeated return to Scripture on behalf of all who ask the twin questions: "What must I do to be saved?" and "What does the Lord require of me?" However, this is not to deny the kinship that preachers have with all creative people, nor that God may move the entire world by the creative impulse that he has scattered abroad.

CHAPTER 2

CREATIVITY AS GOD'S GIFT

Let us embark on a broad piece of speculation. What if the capacity to see is not only the essence and glory of the minister but the growing edge of the whole movement of world history? Suppose God has ordained not just that ministers shall dream dreams and see visions but that people in all professions and occupations shall do the same, from the housewife making a dress to the woman in the state legislature making laws. Could the foreman of a work crew or the painter of a suspension bridge be part of the multitudes meant in the words, "I will pour out my spirit on all flesh; your sons and your daughters shall prophesy, your old men shall dream dreams, and your young men shall see visions" (Joel 2:28)?

This interpretation would, of course, secularize the vision. Normally, the vision of Joel refers to the saving Word of God, and not to just any creative word. It is rightly applied to the Day of Pentecost, when all confinements broke open for the church and the church went everywhere preaching the word. But the spirit that Joel promised is also the Creator Spirit. In the beginning, it brooded over the universal void and brought forth seas and dry land, the galaxies, and all living things. It also brought forth man and woman, with the mandate to subdue the earth. The question we raise is whether all creative power is traceable back to this source.

The Broad Movement of Creativity

For the moment, and without giving "proof" or tracing theological implications, let us opt for the broader interpretation. Let us say that the interests of the Spirit are as broad today as "in the beginning." All seers, in the church and outside the church, in religion and in every secular field, are inspired to create by the hidden power of God. This means that civilization at any moment of time is like a vast front facing and striving with the future. In the past, the road along which the present has moved is dotted with the past accomplishments of the human race. There are "cities" of Greek philosophy, of Renaissance art, of thirteenth-century cathedrals. There are secure fortresses of eighteenth-century political theory, nineteenth-century industrial prowess, twentieth-century science and technology. The front has been advancing through the centuries at an uneven pace, but always in the front line have been the creators. Sometimes they are particularly numerous in one particular sector of the front.

Karl Jaspers notes that from the eighth to the sixth century B.C., the religious front forged ahead. Towering geniuses within a brief period of years pushed the front far ahead in that one field. There were people like Hosea, Amos, Isaiah, Jeremiah, Buddha, Zoroaster, Confucius, Lao-Tzu. But, then, other parts of the line moved up. The fifth century B.C. was a golden age for the humanities: Plato, Aristotle, Pericles, Sophocles. That same front would come alive again in the Renaissance of the fifteenth and sixteenth centuries, making advances through Leonardo da Vinci, Michelangelo, Raphael, Titian, Tintoretto. Then came the age of exploration and territorial advance, later the age of industrial advance, and most recently the great and massive surge of science, each age propelled by its seers. Always, the creators are responsible for the advance, and hold the prospects for further conquest.

What if we took religious words, "where there is no vision the people perish," and applied them to this secular movement of history? What if these words applied not only to ministers intent upon something from the Word of God that can be shaped into a sermon but to ministers intent upon the many words of God that can be shaped into the truth of mathematics, paintings, laws, and commerce? That would bring to our consciousness a much vaster God and a secular but hidden form of the *Corpus Christianum,* of that period when a visible unity of the church was sought. On the surface, this seems like an unholy alliance, to mix the sacred and the secular so intimately. Or it may seem antiquarian, like a return to the religious unities of the thirteenth century, when the tight control of the church was exercised over everything. But we are not speaking now of an organizational church in control. We are speaking of the living God, in ways often past our comprehension, being involved in the creative endeavors of the race. Is it likely that God's work shall be locked up in churches on Sunday morning and not be displayed all along the vast front of civilization *vis-à-vis* the future? Is it likely that all the creative power of insight from God will pour through our laypeople on the stewardship committees or in women's guilds? Surely God has greater purposes than this. What if all the *Eureka*'s that sound from workers in all provinces of civilization are really the many dialects of God and that without these, the people—all people—will perish? That would make all of life sacred, even in those areas where stained-glass windows are out of place. It is this possibility that we are affirming.

Scriptural Foundations for a Broad Conception of Creativity

On what basis can such an affirmation be made? Is this just a nice Pollyanna wish, that God be seen as the hidden power behind all human creativity? Is our speculation as to God's involvement in all areas of civilization akin to the whimsy of the Queen in *Through the Looking-Glass,* who believed as many as six impossible things each day before breakfast? No, this speculation can never be total whimsy for any who take seriously the doctrine of creation and who are willing to give it broader scope than is usually given. We have repeatedly confessed, "I believe in God the Father Almighty, maker of heaven and earth," but we have left the making of heaven and earth too much a past event, unrelated to modern times. Properly the doctrine must tie the past event to a current process. How shall we describe this?

God created. How he created, and why, are mysteries. These twin questions will always be unanswerable. We say, in answer to the first, that God created *ex nihilo,* as if we have said something understandable. But this simply adds mystery to mystery. We sometimes give as a rationale for the creation that God needed an object to love, since love was of his nature. But this doesn't penetrate the darkness either. Perhaps the analogy with creative people is just as helpful. Many creative people confess that their ideas arose *ex nihilo.* They don't usually describe them in Latin. They usually say that their ideas arose "out of the blue" or "from nowhere." They also testify that the idea, once it is born, carries its own inner drive to be expressed, to take the long tortuous road from imagination to creation. Could it be—and here I am speaking absurdly—that the Trinity were one day struck with a grand "Aha!" and they took this unusual idea from all the churning mass of ideas that swirl through the Godhead, and nursed it along until it grew and was clarified, and finally expressed? Simply, that's the way it is. Ideas carry the power of expression, and of disappointment if frustrations prevent the revealing. Therefore, when the earth was without form and void, God was brooding, as Descartes brooded before the fire or Housman on an afternoon walk. Then, up from the celestial table he rose, thumped an everlasting fist, gave a divine smile, and first used the words, "Let there be . . ." And it was so!

What was so? Just an event back there? It is interesting how in the popular mind the term "creation" is left back in prehistory and is usually thought of as an instantaneous happening. Thus, four billion years of world development are skipped over to pay tribute to an instantaneous act of creation. Like the eighteenth-century deists, we let God "make," and then concentrate on evolution as a process that God incorporated, so that the world could roll on by itself. Supposing the original idea in the Godhead to which God said "Aha!" was not just a plan of beginning, but also of completing. Suppose it included the six days by a circuitous route of almost four billion years, and that it also included the last few years of human history, and the ultimate Omega point of completion? And what if God agreed to stand by that plan until its completion? That means God is still working out a plan and running tests, all with the knowledge that the creation is quite

incomplete until the new heaven and the new earth come
to pass "wherein dwelleth righteousness."

The upshot is that in popular parlance we have been
talking about the creation as a past event, when in actual-
ity we should have been talking about the *process* of
creating. We have surrounded ourselves by the limiting
phrase "in the beginning," so that we cannot get past the
gate and look to the final creation. The doctrine of creation for most people who recite the Apostles' Creed begins and ends with Alpha, whereas God is both Alpha and
Omega. Creation has not just happened. It is happening.
And it must be happening throughout the universe, if
that indeed was the broad scope of the original plan God
had when he first created, "in the beginning."

There is a further corrective of the popular mind. Men-
tion God and creation, and not only do we skip over four
billion years of creativity, but then we put blinders on so
that we don't see all peoples and all types of human
activity in our peripheral vision. It is true that God selected Abraham, Isaac, and Jacob; and surely he called his
people out of Egypt; and most certainly "if any one is in
Christ, he is a new creation" (II Cor. 5:17). But what
about the tremendous, all-embracing language of Ephesians? According to Paul's immense thought, those who
are made alive in Christ are not God's end product. They
are part of a movement. They are expressing by their
newfound faith a oneness previously impossible. Paul observed that in the church, the walls were now down. The
hostility of race and sex had ended. A new humanity had
begun. Sometimes Paul refers to this group of believers
as the body of Christ, "the fulness of him who fills all in
all." At other times, he speaks of the church as the temple
of the Spirit, the dwelling of God on earth. But however
grand the church is conceived to be, the thought of Paul

expands until it takes in a scope that is as great as the original creation. A plan has been revealed for the fullness of time, says Paul, to "unite all things in him, things in heaven and things on earth" (Eph. 1:10). If this unity is not to be a dull uniformity, then there is room for all the rich interplay of the human spirit. There must be room in that final plan for more music than church music and for a fuller wisdom than that of the church fathers. If history is the stage where this final unity in Christ will be worked out, rather than by divine fiat or by apocalyptic cataclysm, then it is also possible that God is using the frustrating but exciting process of creativity to accomplish his total ends, even while using the church and the proclamation of cross and resurrection to accomplish his saving ends.

Quite understandably, the language of the Bible gets channeled in our thinking into the all-important theme of salvation. We concentrate as preachers on the mighty acts of God. The language involves Christ and the church, or Moses and the exodus. We use as a matter of course the tradition of exodus and pilgrimage to the Promised Land, and of redemption and pilgrimage to the City of God. But what about the inclusive language of Ephesians, where it is stated that all things in the universe are to be placed under Christ? Even assuming the high place that God has given to the church in the ultimate plan, to the proclamation of the saving word through the sermon, is it conceivable that the full spectrum of life will be left out of a new heaven and earth? Surely something of variety will be present, such as is represented by world religions and international commerce, Japanese art, American politics, Iranian rug-weaving, Caribbean tourism, Indian silver craftsmanship, Alaskan scrimshaw. The word "all" in the phrase "to unite all things in him" must mean "all," and thus be built into the new City of God, or some of the varied colors will be gone. It is a pity, for instance, that the old descriptions of heaven have caused red-blooded, adventuresome people to wish for some other place that was more interesting. The problem was that in focusing on the saving work of Jesus, we did not allow for all the creative enterprises of the race to be present too.

Nothing of what is presented above is meant to minimize the gospel or the church. It is meant to enlarge thought about the bigness of God. No one can read Loren Eiseley, and his ponderings on evolution, without an awesome appreciation of the time phrases in the Bible, such as "in the beginning," "the eternal God is thy refuge," "from everlasting to everlasting." By the same token, conceiving of a world that is ceaselessly being worked on until the final draft is right gives a new appreciation of creation. Creation is then not a static word, reserved for two chapters of Genesis, with an occasional quote from Isaiah 40 or Job 38. It is a constant happening, going on under the noses of every generation, and proceeding until a final "It is finished" can be pronounced.

Where is mankind, where are God's human creatures in this vast panorama? They are always sinners in need of redemption. They are always frightful in their possibilities for evil. They are always free enough to destroy, perhaps to throw the creative line of civilization back to some dark age. But human beings have just as great a potential for good. They can be redeemed, and be part of God's new humanity; but even apart from this, they can unwittingly be God's servants working for a new day. While not necessarily "saved" by Christian standards, they are capable of the awesome "Aha!" of all creators. They think God's thoughts after him. They are always on the border that faces new territory, where their mind ranges over land that has not been traversed before. Some of the land may be distinctively religious, and refer explicitly to Torah and Gospel. But not necessarily so. God's plan sweeps wide. Much of the land to be traversed will be outside the mind of the church's message, though still part of the plan in the mind of God. The thoughts of people as creators are thoughts of goals and how to reach them. They are thoughts that involve frustrated ponderings and mini-breakthroughs; they are thoughts of invention and medical cure, of five-year plans and political platforms. In other words, wherever human beings live, and in whatever times, they live by the possibilities that those times present to them. Every area of life is either making increments of progress toward a new creation or it is creeping backward until some new brooding over some new chaos will bring light and direction. But the brooding is done by the Spirit in the mind of humanity. In the words of an ancient proverb: "Without God, we cannot; without us, God will not."

It was to the earliest men and women that God said, "Subdue the earth." Prior to the covenants and the election of a people, men and women were charged with the obligation to have dominion over all. Having dominion can be interpreted in the idiom of American big business to mean consuming the resources, manufacturing the latest gadget, increasing the gross national product. Or it can refer to a responsible ordering of society and environment under a dream of paradise and a responsibility to God. In any event, it is the human race that figured in God's great "Aha!" And it is the same human race that has been saying its little "Aha!" ever since, making its mini-creations with the sweat of its brow. Jesus said, "As the Father has sent me, even so I send you" (John 20:21).

These words might be paraphrased thus: As I have created you, go forth and be creators too. Every age, in all parts of civilization, in every part of the globe, has this creative task.

Rollo May takes an interesting measure of the artist Pablo Picasso, seeing him over a long period of creativity.[14] The case gives some small hint as to the part that creators play in interacting with the intricate process of world history. Picasso picks up and reflects the spiritual temperament of each age he lives through. In the early works of 1900, he painted starkly realistic canvases of peasants and poor people. There was a passionate relationship to human suffering. In the early 1920's, Picasso was painting classical Greek figures, particularly bathers by the sea. This period after World War I was a time of escapism. The war to end wars was over. The mood was relief and relaxation. At the end of the '20s, the bathers become pieces of metal, mechanical gray-blue curving steel, beautiful, but impersonal and cold. Something ominous was happening in the world. People were becoming impersonal, objectivized numbers. The machine age of production lines and computers was ahead.

Then, in 1937, the great painting *Guernica,* with figures torn apart, stark, white, gray, and black, reflected Picasso's pained outrage against the bombing of the helpless Basque town of Guernica by Fascist planes in the Spanish revolution. In the late '30s and '40s, Picasso's portraits become machine-like; people are turned into metal, faces distorted. It is as though persons, individuals, do not exist anymore. Their places are taken by hideous witches. Significantly, the pictures are no longer named but are numbered. Human beings have lost their faces, their individuality, and their humanity. May concludes:

In this sense, genuine artists are so bound up with their age that they cannot communicate separated from it. In this sense, too, the historical situation conditions the creativity. For the consciousness which obtains in creativity is not the superficial level of objectified intellectualization. . . . Creativity, to re-phrase our definition, is the encounter of the intensively conscious human being with his or her world.[15]

Art is a much easier area in which to see human beings at work as creators, interacting with their times, than is the work of the auto mechanic or the borough council-woman. Almost by definition, artists hold the mirror up to nature. They see so that we can see. They are taken by their environment, and they bring their vision and energy to what intrudes. It would have been as impossible for Picasso to paint *Guernica* for the Crystal Palace of the Victorian era as for Van Gogh to paint like Raphael. The times were moving, and then as always, the artist's environment was the matrix from which the immediately new is born.

Having said all this, we can affirm that even mechanics or borough councilwomen are not debarred from the creative task that lies on the border of their fields. Perhaps their new thing is an improved gadget, or a redesigned part, or a rewritten ordinance, or a better plan for traffic flow. These are not prime features of the new creation, nor worth a line in an encyclopedia. Yet these acts are the increments of creativity that are part of the movement of the world toward the creative ends of God. These *ends* must be stressed as much as *beginnings,* whenever we talk about Genesis 1. No genuinely creative end can be omit-ted from the plan in which God is making all things new.

Marks of God's Activity

But what proof can there be of these assertions? We have drawn some deductions from the doctrine of creation and the theme of Ephesians. We claim that God's creation is never-ending, and that our own human creativity is an expression of God's master plan. We have said that all creators in all walks of life are servants of God, and we use that term "servant" much as the prophets used it of Cyrus or Nebuchadnezzar. We claim that the world and its future belong to the seers. They have to be outside the covenant and strangers to the promise, but they are still lesser lights to lighten the Gentiles. But what confirming evidence is there that this is a proper line of thought?

Perhaps some hints could be garnered from philosophers of history, suggestions that there is a purposeful movement to history. If that could be accepted, even for the eye of faith, then it would be an easy next step to affirm that the shakers and movers of civilizations, the creative spirits, were not totally on their own, but were working within some overarching purpose. Indeed, it is just such a determinism, not necessarily God-directed, that many scholars of history affirm. Predestination is stood on its secular end when men like Hegel, Marx, or Spengler point to the inevitabilities of history. Nothing over all, according to these philosophers, walks with aimless feet. "There's a divinity that shapes our ends, rough-hew them how we will." A few social scientists continue this same line of reasoning, and have shown how many inventions have come to pass as much through the inevitability of the times as through the particular skill of particular geniuses. The discoveries would have happened anyway, according to these scholars.[16] Thus Newton and Leibniz both discovered calculus without any back-room convention of mathematicians. Darwin was quite surprised to learn that Robert Wallace had hit upon the theory of natural selection. The list goes on impressively. Langley and the Wright brothers both invented the airplane; Gray and Bell the telephone; Avogadro and Dalton, the molecular theory; Napier and Bürgi, logarithms; Boyle's law is called Marriotte's law in French textbooks. Perhaps these inventions would have been made if the inventor had died previously, because the chief determinant is the culture and not biology or psychology. These illustrations suggest an inevitable movement to history. Yet they prove nothing. We do not for the moment even evaluate them. They are merely consistent with any claim to purposeful movement, such as we make when we talk about the plan that God had "in the beginning" and that will be brought to completion at the end of time.

Furthermore, even if there is a purposeful movement, no one is quite able to evaluate the advancing trends. Just because there is an explosion called the Industrial Revolution, with genius running wild, does not mean that all such creativity is equally good or consistent with some divine plan. The labor laws of Shaftesbury and Wilberforce seem more creatively Christian than the mogul policies of our American captains of industry, but who can say for certain in every case? There is certainly malevolent creativity in any creative epoch. There is also the real feeling that such evil can easily submerge the more obvious good. Furthermore, no theory of inevitable progress through human creativity can easily be discovered. A turn-of-the-century theory of progress is about as stylish today as spats. It is conceivable that the well of creative impulse will run dry, with God being free to admit that the original plan cannot happen by human creativity. Perhaps after aeons of time and mountains of blueprints, God sadly admits that the plan is unworkable by human means.

Suppose that, instead of advance through creativity, a slow slide takes place back to some barbaric age, where only whiffs of smoke indicate places where cities and homes had been. In this case, the primordial chaos of Genesis would return, and the Spirit would brood over this new void until light appears. This gloomy outlook, adapted as it may be to doctrine, is the view of those who expect things to get worse. The only hope is a completely new creative act by God, a Second Coming. Thus, the late great planet earth will be redeemed, but with human response to God playing little part. These matters we will not debate. If that's the way it will be, so let it be. But, meanwhile, we will continue to fend off the darkness by the act of seeing, until such time as God blows the whistle and calls time. It may just be that when time is called, that will not be the moment of despair, but a proper conclusion. Something about human creativity suggests that through its proper use, God may yet bring about the final plan and keep faith with his own original "Aha!"

Something about human creativity has the mark of the divine. Leaving aside any help that might come from philosophers of history, some insight comes from the creative act itself to suggest the possibility of God's handiwork. I return to my initial experience of running up the stairs and being invaded by the theme of religious imagination. I also return to the invasions of inspiration that propel the weekly sermon. Some comparisons with creativity in other fields start to pop. If my happening was of God (and of this I feel convinced), then enough similarities with the creative experience of others in other

fields might hint that their work is of God too. It is not
that creative people themselves necessarily feel that way.
It is that those standing within the Christian framework,
as the minister-preacher does, may lay claim to soul brothers and soul sisters in the vast plan of God.

For instance, just as in my own case, other people speak
of being grasped initially by an idea that intruded un-
ceremoniously by way of the imagination. The idea had
all the marks of the wind that "blows where it wills." In
recent years, much attention has been given to creativity.
Deliberate attempts have been made to record experiences of gifted people.[17] The usual purpose has been to
study creativity from a psychological or sociological point
of view. Particularly important to educators is this research, to find what factors encourage or inhibit
creativity, what is the relation of creativity to intelligence,
to environment, to curriculum now in use, and so forth.
One interesting thing to notice in these testimonials is
the large number of creative people who confess to flashes
of insight that come spontaneously, and that then guide
the process through to the hard work of creation.

Some of these cases are classic and well known. Rousseau's account is typical. A sudden vision came to him by
the roadside on a hot summer day in 1754 in the course
of a walk from Paris to Vincennes. Among the multitude
of "truths" that flashed upon Rousseau in the preoc-
cupied state into which he fell at the moment was, to use
his own words, "that man is naturally good, and that it
is by our institutions alone that men have become
wicked"—a complete reversal of the church's traditional
doctrine, and of tremendous impact ever since. It is perhaps one of the hidden influences behind *The Greening
of America* and yesterday's flower children. To cite another case: Gibbon, according to his autobiography, sat

musing amid the ruins at Rome. Robed, barefoot friars were singing vespers in the Temple of Jupiter. Suddenly, like a burst of light, the inspiration for his monumental work *The Decline and Fall of the Roman Empire* came to him, its outline vague, its contents as yet unforeseen, and not to be finished until seven years later. Consider Newton, observing in the fall of an apple a new formulation of the laws of gravity; or Spengler, saying in his ponderous *Decline of the West* that the original idea for that work came to him as a young man in a momentary intuition.[18] The list could be expanded. The point is that the language of the initial inspiration is simply a variation of my own experience of being accosted by a compelling idea. One explanation is to posit a multifaceted intrusion of the Spirit of God. It is not necessary for secular people to maintain this. Their work in mathematics or social work will not be improved or diminished if they do. Rather, the positing is an article of faith for one who wishes to see the world under some aspect of eternity.

There is a further hint, quite subjective and yet not without consequence, that God is working out his vast plan through creative people. I remembered that, in my own case, when creativity progressed, the surge of life was present at the same time. This, too, is not a private experience. A broader look reveals what is almost a law of creativity. Whenever creating is in progress, life starts to beat in the womb. New life. When creation is completed, there is joy as in the harvest. The dark side of this exists too. When creating is thwarted or pushed aside deliberately, we settle down to ennui, dull routine, the slow march to death by the beat of a clock. Unless there is the making of something new, then the "same wheel deepens the same rut year after year."

Could it be that all creativity is sacramental? By it, the

grace of life is conveyed. Certainly, for the minister as preacher, the seeing that relates Christ to the complexities of life is lively and life-giving to the seer. "Woe is me if I preach not the gospel." There is no hypothesis in this. It is fact. We are most alive in our act of seeing. But, according to their own testimony, others who are seers in other disciplines know this joy too. The closer they are to the ideas that grab them and demand to be worked out, the more they know the capital "L" of Life. I am not saying they are "saved" in orthodox Christian terms. I am arguing that they are dealing with the same God who is working out a complex new creation on all fronts where human beings operate.

Just a few testimonies. "The moment of insight is exciting," says Bertrand Russell. "It is like quick motoring." Tchaikovsky wrote: "I forget everything and behave like a mad-man. Everything in me starts pulsing and quivering."[19] Beethoven even spoke of himself as experiencing a sort of rapture. At such moments he became, as it were, transformed. Hobbes was so full of eagerness that he carried a pen and inkhorn in his cane that he might not lose a thought along the way. Such people are pulsing with the excitement of discovery. They are caught up in something that beats the clock, gives meaning, extends personality, and enters the land of excitement. There is something uncanny about the power of creativity as a life-giving force. It does no good to argue that there is anguish and anxiety, perhaps pain. Of course there is, even the melancholy of a Jeremiah at times. But ask these people whether it was worthwhile to see what they have seen. Inevitably, the response is that the moment of insight was a high point not to be missed.

By the same token, the movement away from creativity is a movement away from life, which also makes sense if the loving God is involved in the process of creativity. Here again, some testimonies are in order.[20] Gibbon, in his garden in Lausanne, describes fully his feeling of melancholy at the completion of *The Decline and Fall of the Roman Empire.* Similarly, Beethoven, after his greatest symphonic effort, returned lonesome and dejected along the wintry streets of Vienna at night to his disheveled apartment. In another world altogether, Harriet Beecher Stowe, pursuing her work with increasing intensity to the last page of *Uncle Tom's Cabin,* felt that with the death of Uncle Tom the whole vital force had departed from her, leaving a feeling of profound discouragement. One interesting case related by a psychiatrist of the Kübler-Ross team is the ultimate form of the creativity-life connection. He told of a well-known Philadelphia author who had a terminal illness. She was working on a book, but kept putting off writing the final chapter. The reason, apparently, was that the end of that book would signal the death that she could not bear to face.

Thus hints exist, but no proof, that all creativity has a divine mark. The minister-preacher begins with his or her own experience of God's dealing. If he detects the way he was overtaken by an inspiration, and if he remembers the life-giving force with which it developed, then he is in some position to take seriously the broad scope of creativity. Without judging specifics as to what is of God and what is not, the minister-preacher senses that the long line of civilization, which right now faces the future, will advance or recede depending on its seers, of which he is one.

Creativity and Christian Doctrine

But, granting this as a hypothesis, how does it relate to certain doctrines within the Christian faith? Let us consider three, all related to the Trinity.

1. *The Doctrine of God.* The unending problem in the Bible, the problem that seers have in confronting those who cannot see, is how to expand the mind to contemplate the vastness of God. When the law commands us to have no other gods before us, the law is broken as much through the impotence of the imagination as through the sinfulness of the will. God is demoted to a second or third place whenever we lose the capacity to think big thoughts concerning our Creator. At that point, when imagination fails, then we confine God to Sunday or to church events, or even to events in Scripture. Meanwhile the vast purpose of God peeps out from other sources. Little tremors of the Almighty come from the outside, from Baalam and Jethro, from the strange presence of Melchizedek or from Naaman, from the Wise Men or from Cornelius. The tremors give reason to believe there is more activity of God out there, and that it is not just found within the confines of our tradition.

Consider some phases of the Old Testament in which the understanding of God was forced to grow. In Phase I, God was one among many gods, and was located primarily in Palestine. This was Elijah's conception when he called for a contest on Mt. Carmel. There was no doubt in Elijah's mind of the reality of Baal, but only of Baal's power in the homeland of Yahweh. Elijah wanted to prove that Yahweh was the stronger of the two deities. In Phase II, the people grow to understand that Yahweh is not only supreme on his own turf but equally effective in other lands as well. It took the exile to prove this. The Jews in Babylon were led to this new consciousness by Ezekiel. This prophet saw that the throne of God was not anchored in Jerusalem, as everyone thought. Instead, it was on wheels and whirling down the Tigris-Euphrates valley. Once again, however, the Jews of Ezekiel's day thought that other gods were real. The new awareness was simply that Yahweh could handle his people despite their residence in alien lands. Phase III included the magnificent insight of Second Isaiah that not only was God able to battle other gods anyplace, but that the other gods were nonexistent. God was God; purported gods were no-gods.

This spiraling out of the imagination concerning God did not stop in the Old Testament. Those Scriptures end, despite the cosmopolitan views of Jonah and Daniel, with a God rooted in the affairs of Judaism. What of the rest of the world, and of nature, and of the universe? Step by step the growth continued. Paul and Peter declared that God was Lord of the Gentiles. Paul declared that God was sovereign over principalities and powers and "the world rulers of this present darkness" (Eph. 6:12). Carrying this insight even farther, Paul affirmed that the entire creation would experience the glorious liberty of the sons of God. And then, in the fullest insight of all, the book of Revelation declared that Jesus is "King of kings and Lord of lords," with the whole universe subordinate to his purpose, and a new heaven and a new earth within his purview.

If the whole Biblical movement tends toward a breakdown of provincialism, it does no good to participate in new forms of provincialism. If the barrier is up between sacred and secular, or between church and state, or be-

tween Sunday and Monday, or between Christian con-
cerns and world affairs, then we have regressed to some
earlier and inadequate view of God. We may even have
regressed to that early period where the power of God was
in competition with the power of other gods and not
always sure to win. To all the ways in which the modern
imagination fails, we must turn our back so as to capture
or recapture a vision of the bigness of God.

We are attempting to suggest that not only is God
ceaselessly active in the universe; he also works—as a
method of his acting—through the creativity of the
human race. This, of course, remains a speculation based
on deductions from one man's experience of a creative
moment. However, some light might be thrown on the
subject by that intriguing verse in the creation story
which says that man and woman were made in the image
of God (Gen. 1:27). That expression, "the image of
God," has been interpreted in a variety of ways. Obviously it refers to a similarity between God and the human
race. What is the similarity? Many suggestions have been
made by theologians: our speech, our memory, our self-
consciousness, our ability to plan, our moral life, and so
forth. Yet, the most obvious similarity between God and
us is seldom mentioned. We create! This power is what
God has just demonstrated in the creation story. No other
attributes of God have yet been mentioned in Genesis 1,
except God's power to bring order out of chaos. If we are
made in God's image, and we are to subdue the earth,
why not see the likeness in the same power of creativity?
We too brood over the darkness, and, like God, we say,
"Let there be light."

This means that God's creative power will help illu-
mine the creative power of the human race, and also
that the latter will raise hints and suggestions concern-

ing the nature of God. There should be no creative
field in which seers do not have some vocal or inadver-
tent word to say about the power of God within
them. Dorothy Sayers plays on this theme in her book
The Mind of the Maker. [21] She feels that the analogy
between man and God is so close that the act of
creating for the artist, for example, throws light on the
nature of God. An idea in an artist's mind, which
arises *ex nihilo* and then is expressed in a play and
effective for an audience, has a trinitarian stamp upon
it. [22] She protests:

It is to the creative artists that we should naturally turn for
an exposition of what is meant by those credal formulae which
deal with the nature of the creative Mind. Actually, we seldom
seem to consult them in the matter. . . . The artist does not
recognize that the phrases of the creeds purport to be observations of fact about the creative mind *as such,* including his
own; while the theologian, limiting the application of the
phrases to the divine Maker, neglects to inquire of the artist
what light he can throw on them from the immediate appre-
hension of truth. The confusion is as though two men were to
argue fiercely whether there was a river in a certain district or
whether, on the contrary, there was a measurable volume of
H_2O moving in a particular direction with an ascertainable
velocity; neither having any suspicion that they were describing
the same phenomena. [23]

God creates. Man creates. The likeness of each to each
is expressed at that point at the very least. The world is
full of the glory of God, incarnate in human creativity.

2. *The Doctrine of the Holy Spirit.* Inspiration, wherever it happens, gives the appearance of a divine visitation. People who make no claim to being religious use the
language of being grasped, invaded, subdued, made

aware, guided. They sound like people of Scripture, or like Luther encountering the book of Romans. In secular ways, the heavens open and the Spirit descends. It is interesting in this connection that both Luther, seized by the meaning of faith, and Booker T. Washington, seized with the meaning of education for himself and his race, used exactly the same language. When Washington was still a slave, he looked through the door of a Virginia schoolroom, where white children were being taught to read. "I thought I was looking through the gates of Paradise," he relates in his autobiography. This parallels almost word for word the language of Luther. The dove was flying over the mind of a future educator as well as that of a future reformer.

Almost any phase of the ministry of the Holy Spirit has a secular counterpart in the testimony of creative people, particularly as feelings are discussed. People come alive. The wind blows over the valley of dry bones until they live. They experience a wide range of feelings: love, joy, peace—particularly joy, if not ecstasy; and also the dark stirrings of anguish, torment, awe. This same gamut, from ecstasy to anguish, occurs repeatedly in the accounts that creative persons give of themselves.

Then, too, creation is the prime work of the Spirit, according to the Scriptures. The Bible opens with the Spirit brooding over the darkness like a mother hen over an egg. Something is ready to be hatched: the world. In the New Testament, the same Spirit is at work, bringing forth Christians who are described as "new creations." All such language also has its secular counterpart. The world that is created is the secular world, with the implication that it will be the arena of God's activity. The "new creations" in this world are to be activists in it rather than recluses or ascetics. Even some Christocentric expressions in the Gospel of John put on a secular face. For instance, Jesus said, "I have yet many things to say to you, but you cannot bear them now. When the Spirit of truth comes, . . . he will take what is mine and declare it to you." Why should these "things" of Christ be limited to Biblical terms of salvation? Why should they not include the full range of secular truth? When Jesus said, "I am the truth," he did not use adjectives. He did not say "existential" or "saving" or "academic" truth. He left the statement unqualified, "I am the truth," thus allowing some freedom for interpretation.

Some miscellaneous observations could also be made concerning Biblical language of the Spirit, which is capable of a broader interpretation. For instance, in Ephesians Paul says, "And do not grieve the Holy Spirit of God" (Eph. 4:30). There is no elaboration of meaning here, just a phrase to ponder. The context contains a catalog of personal sins. But there is also just enough distance from that context to make the phrase stand on its own. What does it mean to grieve the Spirit of God?

One meaning, certainly, is the possibility of misusing the creative gift. Robert Oppenheimer, director of the Los Alamos project some years ago, felt this possibility keenly while working on the atomic bomb. As a result, he resigned from the project. On July 16, 1945, when the first bomb was exploded in New Mexico, he quoted from the *Bhagavad-Gita:*

> I am become death, the shatterer of worlds;
> Waiting that hour that ripens to their doom.[24]

Oppenheimer would have understood the language of Ephesians, "And do not grieve the Holy Spirit of God." His case raises the interesting problem of whether certain inspirations must not be judged by some higher standard, and even denied on that account. As John once said, "Test the spirits to see whether they are of God" (I John 4:1).

If some creative impulses should be blocked for the sake of humanity, some others are blocked deliberately, which may have deprived the world. This, too, may be a grieving of the creative spirit. Hector Berlioz, the famous French symphonic composer, at one point struggled against a creative impulse and eventually killed it. He suffered poverty and, at the same time, anxiety over his wife's health. One night, there came to him the inspiration for a symphony. It rang in his ear, an allegro in 2/4 time in a minor key. He rose from his bed and began to write. But, he thought:

"If I begin this bit, I shall have to write the whole symphony. It will be a big thing, and I shall have to spend three or four months over it. That means that I shall write no more articles and earn no more money, and when the symphony is finished, I shall not be able to resist the temptation to have it copied . . . (an expense of a thousand or twelve hundred francs). . . . I shall have a concert, and the receipts will barely cover the cost. . . ." These thoughts made me shudder, and I threw down my pen saying: "Bah, tomorrow I shall have forgotten the symphony."

But the next night I heard the allegro clearly and seemed to see it written down. I was filled with feverish agitation. I sang the theme. I was going to get up, but the recollections of the day before restrained me. I steeled myself against the temptation and clung to the thoughts of forgetting it. At last I went to sleep, and the next day, upon awaking, all remembrance of it had indeed gone forever.[25]

Who is to judge Berlioz? Does the world need another symphony, or does a wife need a less self-absorbed husband? The incident is cited to present the possibility of blocking a gift, of denying a creation. The Spirit can be grieved, to use Paul's term.

Another observation might also connect the Spirit with the broader reaches of creativity. The Spirit is the prod to adventure. The Bible is full of people setting out on a pilgrimage. They break with the old and end up on the road. They don't know where they are bound, only that there is somewhere a "city which has foundations." Biblical people at best are restless. They confess that they have no abiding place. They know that "there remains a sabbath rest for the people of God," and they seek it, but meanwhile they journey and learn to live with the restlessness. The pilgrimage takes a certain courage. Familiar cities such as Ur and Sodom, Tekoa and Nazareth, have their own settled patterns. The familiar is comfortable. People live and die in those cities, just as their ancestors have done. But to the adventuresome few, the Spirit says: Get up and get out. And those who do it break the patterns and face the wilderness, trusting only their inner voice and the possibility of a Promised Land.

Erich Fromm uses the analogy of birth in discussing creativity, but the mark of venturing forth is obvious. A creative person, says Fromm, is willing to be born and leave the womb of security and nourishment. Creativity is an act of faith and the acceptance of risk. It is an act fraught with guilt, since by nature the creative person is breaking old patterns that have been developed by respected teachers and friends. And yet, something beckons. Here are Fromm's words:

The willingness to be born—and this means the willingness to let go of all certainties and illusions—requires courage and faith. Courage to let go of certainties, courage to be different and to stand isolation; courage, as the Bible puts it in the story of Abraham, to leave one's own land and family and to go to a land yet unknown. Courage to be concerned with nothing but the truth, the truth not only in thought but in one's own feelings as well. This courage is possible only on the basis of faith. Faith, not in the sense in which the word is often used today, as a belief in some idea which cannot be proved scientifically, or rationally, but faith in the meaning which it has in the Old Testament, where the word for faith *('emuna)* means certainty; to be certain of the reality of one's own experience in thought and in feeling, to be able to trust it, to rely on it, this is faith. Without courage and faith, creativity is impossible.[26]

Fromm blends Biblical images with the normal, everyday need to follow the truth. Call it faith, as he does; or call it the need to follow the Spirit. In any case, the position of creative people, the seers, is somewhere out on the road between Egypt and Zion. There is no resting place, only pilgrimage under the guidance of the Spirit.

3. *The Doctrine of the Incarnation.* The theological concept of incarnation has been bent out of shape by being forced into impossible forms. Anything down to earth, practical, and vivid can be called incarnational, simply because to be incarnate means to take on flesh. In a general way, any creation, even of a not-so-vivid, practical sort, can be called loosely an incarnation of the idea that prompted it. The very fact that something has seen the light of day and can be read, or touched, or listened to, means that an incarnation has happened. But this is to use language loosely. The power of the word derives from the birth of Jesus. The part of the master plan in the mind of God that relates to the redemption of the human race was finally actualized. The millions of years of prehistory passed, so too the centuries of human his-

tory, and the fullness of time came. God sent his Son. God was in Christ reconciling. At long last, the elusive Word of God was put where our eyes could see and our hands could handle it. To speak about incarnation in any Biblical sense and to relate this to the total created-creating world, we must touch base with this central fact. Otherwise we give the word "incarnation" a meaning that does not properly belong to it.

In the prologue to John's Gospel there remain some possibilities for interpretation whereby God's creative activity in his human creatures might be traced. For instance, consider the familiar words that tie Christ to the creation: "All things were made through him, and without him was not anything made that was made. In him was life [or, as *The New English Bible* phrases it, "all that came to be was alive with his life"], and the life was the light of men. . . . The true light that enlightens every man was coming into the world." (John 1:3, 4, 9.) This section of the prologue uses light as a synonym for Jesus Christ, and it asserts that the Christ was always active, even before Bethlehem. The primary focus of the light is the salvation of humanity. The aim of the incarnation was obvious—that we should become the children of God (cf. John 1:12). Presumably, any effect of this light in touching human lives before Bethlehem would, in a primary sense, awaken the world to this salvation. Yet, without denying this, we can say that there is a mysterious vastness to images of life and light. All truth, even where it may not be saving truth, is life and light. We speak in a general way of the Dark Ages over against the Enlightenment. We also speak of the lively arts, the lamp of learning, an enlightened mind, life-giving science. Rather than take an either-or position on just what the life and light of the Christ might mean, why not include both? Even before the incarnation, the life of God in Christ was touching men and women both for salvation and enlightenment.

A further thought concerning the prologue to John relates to our subject. Jesus is called by the title "the Word," a title he carried from the beginning. What is a word, any word, but a means of expression? By words we express our minds. The stony silence and the blank stare are broken by words. Communication takes place. Intentions are expressed, purposes defined, and commands given—all by words. In the ultimate sense, the mind of God is revealed by words. To people who need these words, they come as good news from a far country.

Is this word sacred only? Is God's concern only the Word of salvation? Salvation is the Bible's big Word, and for centuries we have been trying to penetrate it so as to proclaim it properly. But, again, is the vast, dynamic Word of God for our salvation a big enough view of what God wants to express? Surely God has a mind for mathematics, or a new invention, or pollution control. If Genesis 1 wants to push out the boundaries of all our human limitations, then God cannot be limited to the Judeo-Christian time track, nor even to world religions as religions. We must entertain the possibility that God has a few secular interests, and not in the same way that a minister might take a day off to go to the ball game or work in the backyard. The secular world is God's full-time concern.

Where does all this leave minister-preachers in relation to all the creative enterprises of the race? Do they operate off on back streets in a world where, as many feel, there are "too many churches and too few chop houses"? Not in the least, unless a minister has such a low view of the vocation that he or she is walked on by public opinion.

The ego strength of preachers is not very great, unfortunately. They are too easily intimidated by other areas of the creative front that seem to bustle with activity. But the worth of the minister's ability to see is not dependent on external policy decisions, nor is it determined by a popularity contest. Jeremiah and Amos were voices in the wilderness, and by external ratings they would have been put off the air. No, the worth of the minister's vision, mixed with all the other visions, is life-giving for the seer and for the world for which the seeing is done.

Let us use once again the analogy of a battle line, where all humanity's divisions are in different sectors of the front: artistic types, scientific types, business types, craftspeople, statesmen, politicians, lawyers. Name the type and give it some part of the front line. Assume that the line faces a future which holds the promise of the Kingdom or the threat of chaos. Neutrality is not possible, only some kind of movement for weal or woe. Also, let us affirm the Biblical idea of the sovereignty of God. God is the creator of the ends of the earth. God holds the world at all times in his hands, as his mind continues to brood over the original plan. The plan, begun in the beginning, is still in the process of being carried out. The ultimate aim is a total world that will be an environment over which God can say, "That's good." It is a world that is to be inhabited by people of a new order, too: new creatures in Christ Jesus.

What part do ministers play in this? Obviously, they have no more technical knowledge than others; nor are they judges of good and bad creations in all fields. But they do function at their best in promoting the new humanity. By telling the gospel story, and sounding the contemporary overtones, they call for repentance and commitment to God. They also, particularly in days of cynicism and despair, hold out hope for the human enterprise. They may take the lead in opening worship up to a larger celebration of creation than ever. Just as Emerson greeted Walt Whitman as a new voice in the land, or as Degas recognized that Mary Cassatt was a kindred spirit, so the preacher may be instrumental in recognizing the hand of God in all creative persons of earth. At that point, a new meaning is put into the Doxology, "Praise God, from whom all blessings flow."

Chapter 3

A GREAT COMPANY OF SEERS

The Old Testament has the word "seer" tucked away as an alternative title for prophet. At first glance, the title seems fortunate, since it has the idea of religious imagination built in. Yet the title may not be such a wise choice after all. A cursory look at the Old Testament shows some strange phenomena attached to the seer. Sometimes he acted like a whirling dervish, dancing ecstatically and kicking his heels. At other times, he exercised the power of clairvoyance. For instance, Samuel was acting like a seer when he told of the finding of Saul's father's lost asses (I Sam. 9:20). When Saul left Samuel, he met some other seers who danced him down to the ground under the spell of the Spirit. All of this activity seems strange, particularly when added to those occasions when seers predicted what would happen many years hence.

Clairvoyance is not exactly a gift exhibited in mainstream Christianity, nor is telling the future through a crystal ball the special talent of modern ministers. A few modern seers seem to know the details concerning "the last days," and a few more might confess to having had a visit with Jeane Dixon; most, however, have no desire to be either an Edgar Cayce or a Nostradamus. Therefore, it is almost a relief for modern preachers to find the crucial text in the Old Testament, "He who is now called a prophet was formerly called a seer" (I Sam. 9:9).

This text suggests that up to a certain point the Old Testament leader was called a seer and that after that time the term "seer" was no longer used. The suggestion is also present that the strange excesses of seers disappeared. This change seems more to our taste, particularly when the prophet is defined as "one who speaks forth," and not as "one who tells fortunes." With that change, we seem to have the model for the modern minister. He is, according to this text in I Sam. 9:9, a prophet and not a seer. He speaks on issues with the conscience of a godly person. He does not dance up a storm or lose his dignity. This sounds good, until a second look reveals that the I Samuel text is not conclusive.[27] No clear-cut chronological division is possible between seers and prophets. The prophets who spoke and wrote after I Sam. 9:9 often did crazy things; they were not above speaking about the future; and they certainly were seers. The Book of Amos, for instance, was written long after I Sam. 9:9, and yet it begins, "The words of Amos . . . , *which he saw.*" If the term "seer" was no longer being used, nevertheless "seeing," or vision, continued with Amos and others like him (cf. Isa. 2:1; Micah 1:1).

Old Testament Seers at Work

Since, then, it is appropriate to call later Biblical prophets "seers," it may be permissible to call the still later modern preachers by the same title. The title "seer" captures the double function of probing life and times through the power of imagination, and of probing deeply into the purposes of God. This double function certainly characterized all the Biblical prophets. They spoke to the crowds in powerful picture language. They were not afraid of apocalyptic imagery. Even visions and dreams were part of the possibilities they traced before pronouncing the "burden" they felt. They were always reaching for ways to reveal the hidden purposes of God. Let us consider a few examples.

Jeremiah sees an almond tree in early bloom. To anyone else, it is simply a flowering tree, a sign of spring. Jeremiah catches a deeper signal. The Hebrew word for "almond tree" is *shaqed*, similar in sound to another Hebrew word, *shoqed*, which means "watching." The almond tree reminds Jeremiah that God is on the watch, on the alert, and ready to carry out his purpose. In another situation, Hosea is embroiled in a difficult marriage. An unfaithful wife, unhappy with normal home life, runs off to have an affair. That fact should have ended the marriage, but, strangely enough, the love of Hosea for his wife will not end. He still wants her back. Then the religious imagination of Hosea is triggered in that he sees the connection between his experience and God's continuing love for His unfaithful bride, Israel. God was saying to Israel just what Hosea was saying to his wife, "How can I give you up?" Again, the seer is at work.

Amos walked down the road to Bethel. A roadside stand was selling day-old fruit and vegetables. Something inside said, "Amos, what do you see?" "A basket of over-ripe fruit [in Hebrew, *qayits*]," he answered. In that instant the inner light flashed. "The end [a similar-sounding Hebrew word, *qets*] has come," he predicted. His sermon came forth as a message of doom, once the original impulse caught hold of his imagination. In the same way Amos also saw a carpenter working on a house, using a plumb line. The carpenter wanted to see if the wall was straight. In his imagination, the house faded and reappeared as the nation. The wall of his nation was out of plumb. Once again, his message to Bethel was caught and conveyed imaginatively. He thereby warned the nation to repent and measure up to the plumb line of righteousness that God was holding.

Assuming that Amos was inspired when he wrote these things, are modern preachers any less inspired if they see in one of these figures a perfect message for their nation? Perhaps the distinction between one kind of inspiration, that of the Bible, and another kind of inspiration, that of sensitive preachers, is not so easy to draw. Bible times and our times may be simply two eras in which the same kind of seeing is done. The seeing that occurs is equally valid, equally rooted in a similar transcendent source, and in a similar Scriptural tradition.

One common mistake that is made by many preachers is to draw too sharp a distinction between the makers of Scripture and the later interpreters of Scripture. According to this view, Amos is a maker of Scripture who is in a class by himself, whereas we in modern pulpits are only interpreters of Scripture. This view is a half truth. The half that is in error fails to realize that Amos had to reflect on the Scripture at his disposal and relate it to new times in much the same way that we do today. That is, the interpretation of Scripture was a continuing process within the canon just as it is a process today. The councils that determined which writings were to be included in the Bible set apart those which contain the story of God's salvation as well as examples of homiletical reflection on this story. The reflections that were going on in Amos were approved by the church, but that fact of approval does not make Amos' reflections different in kind from those of modern preachers. While there might be only one exodus out of Egypt, there are countless ways in which the meaning of the exodus is seen by seers, both inside and outside the canon.

Let us return to the image of the plumb line. We ponder this image in relation to America today. God's straight line, the basis for nation-building, is held in our mind's eye over against the way it is seen in Washington and in state capitals. In fact, unless the modern preacher faithfully sees Amos in the context of the modern day, it may be impossible to appreciate Amos' work in his own day. This places a great responsibility on the modern preacher as one who wears the mantle of prophetic imagination. The responsibility is heightened because it may not be evident until the prophetic moment whether a word to the nation should be the judgment of Amos or the mercy of Hosea. At certain times in our national history, such as when Kennedy or King died, or when Watergate festered, the plumb line was clearly visible to the eye of faith. It stretched from heaven to earth, with the plumb bob alongside Washington and every city in the land. Everything at that time seemed out of plumb. It was easy to preach a message of judgment. Yet during the Bicentennial celebration, the tenderness of Hosea was the dominant theme of many prophets. We needed to hear, "How can I give you up?" Without that, we could wallow in national guilt and self-pity. In the short time between the Watergate affair and July 4, 1976, the pendulum seemed to swing between woe and weal. Interestingly enough, Hosea and Amos were contemporaries who spoke to the same nation, yet both had a different perspective that rested on their different experiences and their refusal to give a stereotyped message.

A further question! If the modern preacher strikes out on his own, informed by the Scripture tradition but not bound to it, is he or she not still preaching the Word of

God? The word might be different in degree and emphasis, but is not different in kind. For instance, suppose in going down a street in a modern town you see the first phase of a building in which a steel staircase rises up into the sky with no building around it. The message can be varied, allowing for the free play of imagination. It can be, "All Set Up and No Place to Go." This sermon could stress the futility of modern living. It could have Amos as its text, in that Amos saw in his times all the accouterments of religion but not the reality of God's presence. Or the theme could be, "Get the Steps in Place Before You Build." Here a Jeremiah text would be used, "Return to the Ancient Paths." Or the theme could be, "Let's Get On with It," with the sermon being a challenge to complete the job. The prophet Haggai would understand this vision, since he wrestled with a situation in which everybody built his own home and forgot to build the Temple of God.

In all three cases, the initial image, a modern building under construction, functions exactly like Amos' plumb line or roadside stand. What is spoken seems to be every bit as much the Word of God as what Amos said to his people. This gives a continuity to the Word of God. Whereas we often think of that word as confined within walls of ancient Scripture, in modern preaching the wall would come down. That which we share with the oldtimers is a God-inspired imagination. This is the prophet's mantle, which comes upon the prophets' sons and daughters.

Seers and the Doctrine of Inspiration

One question, however, arises concerning the doctrine of inspiration. Is there not a great difference between the modern preacher and, say, Amos? The very word "inspiration," which we have been using at times interchangeably with "religious imagination," has a unique ring when applied to canonical books. Those books are inspired in a way that no other books have been inspired. "All scripture is inspired by God and profitable for teaching, for reproof, for correction, and for training in righteousness" (II Tim. 3:16). This was not said of the philosophy of Plato or the plays of Sophocles. If ministers are inspired when they work at sermonizing, and all creative people are likewise inspired, that is one level of meaning of inspiration. Bible writers and prophets are in a class by themselves, however, set off within the wall of the canon. They are uniquely inspired, the rest of us are not.

This interpretation, which is a common one, needs to be challenged. Unless it is, we as modern seers will never have a close kinship with our ancestors within the canon. If their calling and proclamation is of an inspiration different from ours, then, by so much, we are second-rate interpreters of the message of God. For instance, when Michelangelo started out, he did what other budding artists did. He attached himself to an established shop. The master of the shop sketched out the main figures of the fresco, while the apprentices filled them in. The real inspiration was in the master. The apprentices only imitated. By the same token, unless the preachers of today have equal inspiration with the canonical preachers, then we have no more creativity than to flesh out the figures the early masters have drawn. But this would lower the high calling of the preacher. No one wants to work slavishly in the Scripture "shop" unless he has power to do some work on his own.

Fortunately, some recent scholarship has been done on the subject of Biblical inspiration which reveals that inspi-

ration was never a criterion in early centuries to block off
Scripture writings from other writings.[28] It is not that the
Bible writers were not inspired. It was assumed that they
were. The main point is that their inspiration rushes right
past the wall of the canon, past the book of Revelation
and New Testament times, and falls on those outside the
canon as well. Albert Sundberg argues this point effec-
tively and gives ample testimony from the church fathers
to substantiate his belief. He notes that the New Testament testimony itself reveals that inspiration can never be
locked up within the New Testament. Throughout the
New Testament, the consistent teaching is that God has
poured out his Holy Spirit on *all* believers in Jesus. Paul
taught that no one can say "Jesus is Lord" except by the
Holy Spirit (I Cor. 12:3). In Acts, Luke related to all
believers in Jesus the promise of the prophet Joel, "And
in the last days it shall be, God declares, that I will pour
out my Spirit upon all flesh" (Acts 2:14–21, 38f.; cf. Joel
2:28ff.). Sundberg declares that he knows of no teaching
in the New Testament that in any way restricts the doctrine of inspiration to particular persons or to particular
times. Into the fourth century, throughout the history of
the canonization of the New Testament, the church
knew of no restrictions of that doctrine, either to apostles
and prophets, or to apostolic times.

The Christian doctrine of inspiration, therefore, could
not serve as a criterion of canonization. This was not
because the inspiration of Scripture was in any doubt, but
because the doctrine of inspiration was so broad in the
church as not to be limitable to the canon of Scripture.
Sundberg gives a large number of examples that prove his
point. One must suffice here. Just as we would expect, one
of the earliest Christian writings outside the New Testament, I Clement, says of Paul's first letter to the Corin-

thians, "Take up the epistle of the blessed Paul, the Apostle. . . . With true inspiration, he charged you concerning himself and Cephas and Apollos." This letter shows that Paul's own sense of inspiration was also attributed to his letters by his earliest Christian readers. But what is not expected is that Clement speaks of his own writings in the same way. He writes, "You will give us joy and gladness if you are obedient to the things *written by us through the Holy Spirit.*" Certainly in this letter the Holy Spirit is not thought to be bottled up in a canon. The Spirit moves in all Christians. And if in Clement, why not in all preachers, including those of modern times?

We must learn to separate the doctrine of inspiration from too exclusive a tie to the canon. That is, we must stop thinking of the canon as the sole repository of inspiration. The canon, which is the word the church used to designate its accepted books, means "the measure" or "the standard." In forming the canon, the church acknowledged and established the Bible as the standard of inspiration in the church, not as the totality of it. What concurs with the canon is of like inspiration; what does not is not of God. Thus, the Christian doctrine of inspiration describes the unity of Christians with their canon. The Spirit of God that inspires these books dwells in and enlivens them. But Christian inspiration parallels Biblical inspiration, complementing it and opening every Christian age to theological verisimilitude. Sundberg concludes his essay on how the Spirit keeps springing out of the confines of the canon so as to seize the imagination of the long train of post-Biblical thinkers. He says:

The Christian doctrine of inspiration encourages the Christian, to paraphrase Henry Cadbury, neither to run the peril of modernizing Jesus, nor of archaizing ourselves. Rather, the Christian doctrine of inspiration, drawn from the New Testament and Christian thought from the period of Bible canonization, is that the Christian embodies the living and enlivening Spirit of God in every age for that age, the Bible canon being the standard, the measure of all things. "The letter kills, but the Spirit makes alive."[29]

This fact is cause to celebrate our identity with Biblical seers. They and we are soul brothers and sisters who know the excitement of being alive to God. Together, we intuit the connections between where they are and what God had done, and what is demanded. We read surface history only to be triggered into some deeper meaning. Seers know what my feeling was in running up the stairs, or Newton's in seeing the apple fall, or Wordsworth's in stumbling onto a field of daffodils.

The broadening of the doctrine of inspiration raises an interesting question. How is the kinship to be conceived between the modern Biblical preacher and the vast number of creative people in all other provinces of civilization? Have we not run the danger of reducing Scripture to the same common level of inspired poems and novels, paintings and programs? Not only is Amos linked to modern preachers, but both are linked to scientists and statesmen. Is this view not too broad? Does it not take the protective wrapper from Scripture, thus allowing it to spoil? If all creators and creative writings are inspired, then what is special about what we do as preachers? In an effort to see soul brothers and sisters within the canon, perhaps we are deluged with too many creative cousins from all of world history.

The answer to this criticism must go back to the two distinctives of religious imagination that were mentioned in Chapter 1, that set off religious imagination from imagination in general. Religious imagination makes Scripture the glass of vision. These distinctives put Biblical preachers in the immediate family with modern preachers, whereas other creators are only second cousins. In the canon, God acted in a saving way. Events took place at the Red Sea, at Sinai, at Bethlehem, and at Jerusalem which special seers knew were God's saving acts. The record of these and the interlocking interpretations of their meaning became Scripture.

The continuing proclamation of these same events and whatever new meanings flash forth are of the same genus. The modern proclamation is even called the Word of God, for by it—by "the foolishness of what we preach" —God continues to save those who believe, just as he did when the same kind of preaching took place within the canon. Therefore, though all creative people rest on inspiration, ministers in and out of the canon have a special assignment within the whole. They wish to track God's ways so that the world might not get lost. To do this by sticking to the story of God's prime activities is both a limitation and a liberation. Such a dogged persistence with Scriptural events simply proves that when the eye of faith is turned repeatedly on Torah and Gospel, it is not long before the entire universe is under view, and the purposes of God are vaguely etched on the landscape. Therefore, we must hold to the distinctives of religious imagination, even while we realize that other types of imagination, also inspired by God, are at work in the complex movements of history.

The Process of Seeing in the New Testament

Let us now return to the kinship of Biblical seers and modern seers. What often prevents the realization of the basic connection is a blindness to the process of seeing that is going on within the canon. We falsely assume that Scripture was sewn ready-made into the covers of a book we call the Bible. We make the error of treating the Bible as a static entity, thinking that the process of interpretation belongs to us. The Bible becomes a congealed revelation under this misconception. Yet nothing could be farther from the truth. The process of seeing and the growth of revelation is churning within the canon—the same process in which we are engaged. Strange as it sounds, Scripture writers interpreted their Scripture to their audiences. These writers and preachers faced old texts and new situations until new revelations occurred. They too needed to make Scripture a glass of vision and use it in the same way that we today turn to their writings for texts and interpretations. Nowhere is this process more obvious than in the New Testament itself. Let us, therefore, turn to the New Testament for some examples of this process in operation.

Have you ever been impressed by the looseness with which the New Testament writers quote the Old Testament to back up their position? There is an imaginative connection, not a close point-by-point congruence. The prophecies are not fulfilled with exactness. The identities are not of the order of precedents which an attorney presents to the court. In fact, without the eye of faith, the connection could be missed entirely. This is not to criticize the writers' use of the Old Testament. It is to say that by quoting the Old Testament, the New Testament writers are showing continuity suggestively, not definitively. They are using the mentality of a seer rather than that of a meticulous scholar.

Consider the well-known quotation in Matthew about the virgin birth:

All this took place to fulfill what the Lord had spoken by the prophet:

"Behold, a virgin shall conceive and bear a son,
and his name shall be called Emmanuel."

(Matt. 1:22–23)

When you examine this text in the Isaiah context, the miracle has nothing to do with parthenogenesis, no matter how you translate the Hebrew word for virgin. In Isaiah, a king who is unfaithful in his foreign policy, who is all wrapped up in mundane affairs, who takes an "I know best" attitude toward God, is being told that a pretender will be born in his lifetime, in whose time God will act. The old order, the chief concern of Ahaz, was to give way to the new. A new birth would be the signal for the death of the old and the birth of the new. The sign of the birth would thus be a gauntlet laid down, with a gift in it.

How odd that we have argued through much of the twentieth century about whether the virgin birth really happened, when the imaginative point of identification is that the old order of the first century, and of our century, is now under indictment. We who participate in that order like Ahaz, who feel religion has no right to change it, who want to establish it forever to our own advantage, are going to be undermined by a birth that God slips in under our noses. A legalistic mind debates method; an imaginative mind sees the deeper connection.

Paul, who has the same theological idea that Christ broke the old order to start a new creation, does not once refer to the virgin birth. Assuming that he knew of the virgin birth, as he walked the imaginative trail through past history, he did not collect and use this piece of argument. Yet, he does come up with Scripture that is just as loosely interpreted as Matthew's, and just as effective. For instance, he writes:

"Rejoice, O barren one who does not bear;
break forth and shout, you who are not in travail;
for the children of the desolate one are many more
than the children of her that is married."

(Gal. 4:27)

The quotation is from Isaiah, but the meaning for Isaiah is not some far-off New Testament event. He is speaking to a nation that feels like a barren woman, with no future. The situation reflects the attitude of his nation during exile. However, Isaiah insists that miracle births will occur. The nation will have a host of children. A bigger and better tent will be needed to house them all. Instead of a virgin birth, Paul speaks of a post-menopause birth. Both births are tied to Christ. Both Paul and Matthew use the Old Testament tradition; however, the tie is an imaginative connection, not a logical argument. You must be a seer to get or perceive the connection. Is this not the way any serious preacher reaches back to the tradition to make his point? Suggestively?

The same imaginative connection can be observed in the way the New Testament uses the tradition. Let us assume there is a corpus of the mighty acts of God that includes not only the life, death, and resurrection of Jesus, but a continuity with the past events of patriarchs—passover, exodus, Promised Land—then forward to the mighty acts that would sum up the last days and the new aeon. A casual reading of the sermons in the book of Acts will reveal that these same elements come up again and again. However, the way they are slanted, the significant omissions, and the conclusions that are drawn mean that it is not the stereotype of the same story at all. The jewel

appears in different settings. For instance, the long sermon of Stephen in Acts 7 may look like a straightforward
presentation of Jewish history. It is factual, historical, a
résumé of God's bringing a people to birth. However, in
almost every scene, the emphasis is upon the Jewish resistance to the plan of God, which Stephen was feeling
as the word to be spoken at that moment. The Jews are
the "stiff-necked people, uncircumcised in heart and
ears" (Acts 7:51), and he repeats the refrain. Was this
aspect in the original story? Yes, but not in so condensed
and highlighted a form. The preacher is eliciting the twin
response: "I've heard that before," together with, "What
kind of deliberate twist is he giving our history?"

Two more brief examples will show how the Old Testament tradition is adapted. Implicit meanings in the Old
Testament, never seen by those ancient authors, are
picked up in the New. It is as if those in the new era who
found Jesus Christ, and who believed he was as great an
event as anything God ever did, found hidden meanings
popping up all over the place, pleading for a new voice.
For instance, the angel's announcement to Mary about
the anticipated birth is a great declaration on its own.
"With God nothing will be impossible" (Luke 1:37). Yet
its root is back in the Old Testament story of the birth
of Isaac, where a similar word was spoken: "Is anything
too hard for the LORD?" (Gen. 18:14). In both accounts,
the similarities are striking: an angel visitor, a miracle
birth, the unbelief of the parents, the promise of salvation. The half-filled meaning of a story back there is
picked up and redirected for a new era.

Similar things could be said of the Magnificat (Luke
1:46–55), or even of the Benedictus (Luke 1:68–79). The
Magnificat is an update of the song of Hannah in I
Samuel 2. In the Old Testament setting, just as in the

New Testament, it is a time of spiritual dullness. Eli and his sons are in power. The epitaph *Ichabod*, "The glory has departed" (I Sam. 4:21), will soon be written. Again, a miracle birth takes place. God did it again! Great things are incipient in the birth. The vehicle of a song is in order. The finer points of the language used in the two songs have been compared by Von Rad, showing both the similarities as well as the daring new thrusts.[30] The following expressions bridge both testaments: "God the savior"; "who does great things"; "who visited and redeemed his people"; "and remembered his covenant." Even deliverance from "enemies" reappears (cf. Luke 1:71, 74). But now, in the New Testament, these terms are attached to the celebration of the coming of Jesus Christ. In the process, these phrases do not lose the meaning they had originally. It is still true that God redeems, shows mercy, satisfies his own, etc. Yet there has been some change, a fusion of new meaning in the old, simply because these expressions are put into an entirely new theological perspective. For instance, the concept of man's deliverance from "enemies" has shifted from armies to social problems or to personal problems if not to "principalities" and "powers" and "the world rulers of this present darkness." The old terms will still stand in their first usage, but they will never be quite the same once they have churned through the imagination of a new seer who lives in a new set of circumstances.

Once again, the way the New Testament writers use the Old Testament tradition is the way any preacher tells the story. To do so is not to exercise the singular skill of a scholar. It is to use the artistic sense, to see the connections, to recoin old phrases. The preacher is a seer, just like Amos, just like Stephen. The canon is still the measure that the church has used to mark out the definitive acts of God, the story line. However, the process of telling it breaks out of the canon and keeps the story adaptable to every emerging age.

Even the ethics of the New Testament show evidence of a process rather than a solidified code that is ready-made for application. Consider Paul. It should be obvious that the various situations in which Paul gave advice were not meant to be rules that should be reproduced in all other churches. On the one hand, Paul did not cover all possible church situations. If these were to be the rules of the game, then a great number are missing. On the other hand, many of the cases Paul did cover involved contexts and contained end results that no longer apply. For instance, in I Corinthians, Paul gives a series of ethical admonitions that would give the modern church leader pause. Even where some aspect of the tradition reinforced the teaching, the modern conscience is not convinced. Here is a partial tabulation:

Advice to the unhappily married	Split up if need be, but let there be no remarriage.
Advice to the widows and unmarried	You are better off never marrying.
Advice in case of incest	Throw the offender out of the church.
On taking pay for preaching	It is permissible to take pay, but preferable not to.
On hair styles	No long hair for men. No short hair for women.
On taking cases to court	A Christian should never go to law against another Christian.

| Position of women in the church | The women should keep silence in the churches. |

Some Bible-believing people try to turn the teaching in each of these passages into timeless truths. This becomes a modern legalism that requires memory and guts, but little imagination. Others treat Paul as impossible, and simply ignore his ethical counsel and barbed theology. This type of modern liberalism is perhaps valuable and imaginative, but no longer within the Christian tradition. The alternative is a mediating position in which Paul is seen as creatively applying the gospel story to a host of emerging new problems, with the unwritten assumption that such problems will keep emerging and keep requiring new solutions. What is given in the New Testament is not definitive ethical rules, but a paradigm that requires new application in every generation. It requires a seer as an ethicist.

Let us consider an ethical possibility growing out of the exodus tradition, one that is replayed in the Gospels and is exciting for modern America. The text of Lev. 25:10 reads: "Proclaim liberty throughout all the land unto all the inhabitants thereof." This verse has national significance because it is inscribed on the Liberty Bell. The obvious connection between old times and our times is in the word "liberty." The Hebrew exodus filled the minds of New England preachers and also the minds of our nation's founders. Both Franklin and Jefferson wanted scenes from the exodus on our country's national seal. Jefferson designed the seal showing Israel following the cloud and pillar of fire. Franklin settled on a picture of Moses stretching out his hand over the sea, with the inscription underneath: "Rebellion to tyrants is obedience to God." But there is a deeper meaning to the

Liberty Bell text that no Founding Father would claim.

The setting for Lev. 25:10 is not simply liberty after years of slavery. The theme involves the year of Jubilee, which was an idealistic proposal for handling land distribution in the Promised Land. The year of Jubilee was Israel's unfinished business in that it was never implemented, but its meaning is a haunting idea. When Israel inherited the Promised Land, time was to be divided into 50-year periods, with land value related to a 50-year rhythm. When Jubilee struck, all land reverted to its original owner. The disinherited received their paternity. The unfortunate in business had another chance. The wealthy, whether shrewd, lucky, or malicious, had to let go their holdings. Prior to that 50th-year finale, land had value depending on the time remaining until Jubilee. If there were 40 years to go, that land was twice as valuable as if there were only 20. The reason for this strange arrangement was given in terms of the traditional story of God's saving acts: "The land shall not be sold in perpetuity, for the land is mine; for you are strangers and sojourners with me" (Lev. 25:23).

That fuller meaning of Jubilee indicates a deeper kind of freedom: freedom from greed, freedom from land tyranny, freedom from idolatry, and freedom to God. It was the reminder that nothing is ultimately ours. We must sit loose to possessions. Conduct business, yes. Prosper if possible, but enjoy the land while recognizing that God is ultimately the owner. And be ready that it should be given back, lest you become too attached to it.

This text would be spoken by Jesus, but it reached him through the vision of Isaiah. Isaiah, who also saw its significance, applied the Liberty Bell text to Israel in exile (cf. Isa. 61:1f.). In Isaiah's vision, the captives are going to be released and their cause will prosper. They will exchange tears for gladness. They will rebuild old ruins. They will enjoy the wealth of nations. The eternal covenant will be renewed. The end of the exile would be the year of Jubilee. This message Jesus saw as the meaning of his ministry. When he visited the synagogue at Nazareth early in his ministry, he opened the scroll to Isaiah's sermon and read:

> "The Spirit of the Lord is upon me,
> because he has anointed me to preach good news to the poor.
> He has sent me to proclaim release to the captives
> and recovering of sight to the blind,
> to set at liberty those who are oppressed,
> to proclaim the acceptable year of the Lord."
>
> (Luke 4:18–19)

The reference to "the acceptable year" is really a reference to the year of Jubilee. It is good news to the poor; it means the release of captives. It sets at liberty those who are oppressed. That is Jesus' message and purpose. Bondage is severed. His people sit loose to life and are bound to God as free people. What was promised is fulfilled in him.

A text like this, attached to Exodus and the Christ, and taken as a symbol for the nation, is potent for our time. It is a promise of new life in Christ, and inner freedom. But it is also a judgment on an acquisitive society that still lays land to land and oppresses the poor. There is no freedom while business dehumanizes and customs oppress, and ghettos imprison the young. We have forgotten the Jubilee setting of the Liberty Bell text. Freedom is seldom attached to land reform, zoning policy, or fair taxation. Ultimately, it is attached to a "sit loose" feeling in all who are conditioned by the habits of acquiring at any cost. Proclaim liberty in the land! This is hardly a favorable or "sweet" message to a land which in historic fact, in its famous line in the Declaration of Independence, came near listing as unalienable rights "life, liberty, and property."

We have considered some aspects of imagination in the canon as compared to the imagination that drives the minister-as-seer. The proposition has been made that a similar spirit is at work on both sides of the canonical wall. We have maintained that in the early church, the doctrine of inspiration was never the criterion of what books should be in the canon. Scriptures were inspired, but so were Christian writings outside the canon. By the New Testament's own validation, Moses' wish had been realized. All God's people were prophets. The Spirit was given to them all (cf. Num. 11:29). With this premise always in the background, we looked within the canon to notice the flexibility of interpretation there. Imagination was working incessantly upon the fact of God's redemption. The purpose of our excursus was to affirm that the process of creativity within the canon is of the same sort as that which the preacher exercises outside the canon. The Biblical seers are not unique. They are soul brothers and soul sisters with all of us who are prompted by the same Spirit of God.

Criteria for Evaluating Seers

A critical question has been raised. How can one distinguish legitimate seeing from nonsense? In the Bible, the question would be phrased, "How can we separate true from false prophets?" On which side of the line would you place Rev. Ike or the Maharishi? Who really speaks for God? How can you tell if your own imaginative aspect of personality is functioning correctly? If all the *Peanuts* cartoon characters are looking at cloud formations, and three of them see wonderful aesthetic shapes, and delight to call them out, whereas Charlie Brown only sees "a ducky and a fishy," who is to say which one is right?

This is not only a problem for the religious use of imagination. Novelists, painters, sculptors, policy makers, and business executives have the same problem. It is the older question of Pilate, "What is truth?" The matter is further complicated; the rules by which judgments are made are not always clear. Business executives can be judged by the profits they generate, and an executive who becomes too humanitarian, too employee-oriented can lose his job, however imaginative his program might be. Even here, however, the application of the criteria is not easy. The criterion of profit-making might be short-sighted policy. What gives a good profit this year might deplete reserves next year, or saturate a temporary market, or fail to promote the research for diversification. How much more difficult are the criteria for judging whether a specific painting is a good painting, or a specific book a good novel.

Most leaders in the religious field appeal to the Scripture story. They let their imagination play upon it and direct it to a contemporary situation. Do they do this authentically? When the social pronouncement bases its rationale on theology, is this really a legitimate use of theology? Is my reference to the Jubilee story in connection with modern America a legitimate use of an old tradition? When a sermon begins with the Scripture reading and proceeds to three points, did the sermon really grow out of what preceded it in Scripture? When we state our latest program and reinforce it with the phrase, "This is Biblical, you know," did the creative mind bring the various elements together under the direction of the

Spirit of God? The question of truth is a perplexing one. It has no final answer.

We who try to do God's work must operate in accordance with the highest insights we possess and leave the result of our efforts to God. The answer will be much the same for all creative people, unless the field is one that has clear, pragmatic answers. Most times, the products of creative minds are not measurable, and it may seem disconcerting to imply that firm criteria for judging between true and false, good and bad, are lacking. However, let us hold for a while that answer which is really no answer.

The problem of truth is not a new one. The speakers and listeners of Bible times, Old Testament and New Testament, had to wrestle with the same thing. How can you tell true from false prophets? How can you tell when someone should be accepted or run out of town? The Old Testament developed some definite views on the subject. For instance, there was an ancient threefold criterion that seems strange to us today. Was the message accompanied by signs? Did the prophet abstain from eating and drinking while he delivered the message? Finally, did the prophet go home by a different way than he came? These tests came into operation in the fate of an unknown prophet who went to speak against Jeroboam at Bethel. He gave the message of judgment, and provided the credentials of abstinence, and the accompanying sign. But he was tested by a prophet "friend," who invited him to return to the "friend's" house for refreshments. As a result of his disobedience, the visiting prophet got torn by a lion and killed (I Kings 13). Such tests of authenticity are no longer in use, and thank goodness the resulting judgment has been tempered. What criteria remain?

Another Old Testament criterion was to inquire whether the the prophecy was fulfilled. Did it really come to pass? The author of Deuteronomy uses this standard as if it were irrefutable: "When a prophet speaks in the name of the LORD, if the word does not come to pass or come true, that is a word which the LORD has not spoken" (Deut. 18:22). Likewise, Micaiah ben Imlah subjects his own message and that of his opponents to this criterion of fulfillment. In speaking to Ahab, who wants a blessing before he goes to war, Micaiah denies any blessing. He then reinforces his message with a prediction that can be measured. "If you return in peace, the LORD has not spoken by me" (I Kings 22:28). Again, Isaiah requests that his words be inscribed in a book for a witness in the time to come—that is, as a permanent means of testing the fulfillment or nonfulfillment of his words (cf. Isa. 30:8). The point is made even more forcefully by Ezekiel: "When this comes—and come it will!—then they will know that a prophet has been among them" (Ezek. 33:33).

This criterion may have more validity, but only if that which is to come to pass can be measured. For instance, I remember how in my boyhood there were many apocalyptic sermons preached on the subject of the last days, in which it was affirmed that Hitler was the Antichrist who was to come immediately before the Judgment Day. Fortunately the messengers had other types of sermons they could preach, since a great many of their apocalyptic ones went up in flames in a German bunker along with Hitler. Most prophetic words are not narrowly predictive. There is no specific event which is supposed to come to pass, and therefore verification is impossible. Moreover, those prophecies which do refer to a future event will often have a conditional aspect. They begin with the word "if." It is often difficult to determine whether the condition has been met. If the prediction fails, the reasons why it fails are debatable. Therefore, we cannot be too glib in saying that the fulfillment of prophecy is what indicates which prophecy is of God.[31]

Another test sometimes used to separate true from false prophecy is the promise of weal or woe. Great prophets have been more apt to point out the hard road that must be taken. They promise judgment ahead rather than a thousand dreams come true. On the other hand, false prophets are often crowd pleasers and handshakers. They will be apt to say what their listeners want to hear. They promise peace, prosperity, and an unending supply of vines and fig trees. Therefore, a rule of thumb for determining whether a prophecy is true or false seems easy. If the prophet promises hardship and calls for repentance, he is of God. If he promises the moon, watch out! But even this criterion is complicated. Many of the preserved prophecies of true prophets contain words of weal and woe almost side by side. For instance, consider two prophets, Ezekiel and Second Isaiah, who spoke within fifty years of each other. They address their fellow exiles. Yet one man speaks of judgment, the other speaks of grace.

Here is the situation in Ezekiel. The people feel that if God gave the land of Palestine to Abram when he was but one man, surely he will give the land to them, his descendants who are many in number, even though they are in exile. Ezekiel is not the least bit impressed by this argument. He gives the word of the Lord:

"You resort to the sword, you commit abominations and each of you defiles his neighbor's wife; shall you then possess the land? . . . I will make the land a desolation and a waste; and her proud might shall come to an end; and the mountains of

Israel shall be so desolate that none will pass through." (Ezek. 33:26–28)

When Isaiah addresses these same people shortly afterward, the harshness of Ezekiel is swallowed up in grace. Isaiah also refers to Abraham, and practically endorses the argument that Ezekiel's followers advanced. He gives the word of the Lord as follows:

"Look to Abraham your father
    and to Sarah who bore you;
for when he was but one I called him,
    and I blessed him and made him many.
For the LORD will comfort Zion;
    he will comfort all her waste places,
and will make her wilderness like Eden,
    her desert like the garden of the LORD;
joy and gladness will be found in her,
    thanksgiving and the voice of song."
                                        (Isa. 51:2–3)

Two men of God, Isaiah and Ezekiel, both speak truly, and yet one speaks judgment and the other speaks grace. Therefore, the criterion of weal or woe as a measuring rod to distinguish true from false prophecy is not always accurate. Often men of God speak judgment, but not always. Often men of God speak grace, but not always. It is impossible to say in advance by this criterion what message is of God and what comes from an alien.

What criteria are left? We have ruled out strange Old Testament tests, and the test of fulfillment, and the test of weal or woe. Can we judge a person's imaginative use of the story by the canon itself? Even though the believing community has determined a definite body of literature that has become a standard for presenting the mighty acts of God, we have found that even within the canon there is sometimes great difficulty in knowing who speaks for God. For a while, Jeremiah is not sure whether Hananiah's prediction of success against Nebuchadnezzar is a more accurate word than his own. It is only later, under further leading of the Spirit, that his own insight is reaffirmed (cf. Jer. 28:10–13). In Acts, the church is not quite sure of Paul; Paul is not sure of John Mark; Peter trusts his vision of unclean animals and then later denies the import of it. Therefore, the canon has within it God's people who are struggling to find out what is valid and what is not—the same question that we in modern times have to face. John generalizes, but he may be saying all that can be said so far as criteria of truth are concerned: "Test the spirits to see whether they are of God" (I John 4:1).

A possible test that is often used, consciously or unconsciously, is the stamp of approval of the Christian community. When the church ordains a candidate for the ministry, it says in effect that the person's prime vision is authentic. The church is willing to be exposed to the message that he or she brings. However, how is this an answer to those lonely voices which the community rejects but which may be truly the voice of God? Or, what do we do with those voices which the community accepts but which may not be the voice of God?

By coincidence, I was writing this on the Fourth of July. Dr. James Saunders was preaching at Princeton Theological Seminary, relating an experience in which he and other church leaders went to South Africa for dialogue on apartheid with leaders of the Dutch Reformed Church. December 16 is the South African Fourth of July. The establishment of the nation is told with all the vivid imagery of the exodus, and with all the reverence and the Christian interpretative thrust that surrounds that story. The Afrikaaners, God's chosen people, were being pursued by the British (Pharaoh's army). The chosen ones were backed up against the Blood River, with a host of Bantus on the other side (the Canaanites). At the last minute, some regiments of calvary arrived on the flank (Enter Moses and a small force of the righteous). The Bantus were cut to shreds, while the Afrikaaners were saved and safely crossed the Blood River (Red Sea) and entered the Promised Land. A Voortrekker Memorial Shrine outside Pretoria marks the spot, and religious fervor makes it hallowed ground. Saunders reported that the Dutch Reformed churchmen could not understand why none of this story, so closely paralleling the exodus story, registered on the Americans. And, similarly, the Americans wondered why the voice of prophecy could not get past the religious-patriotic line of defense. The reason can only be that the authentic voice of prophecy is not always judged authentic by the hearers, even where they have been conditioned by the same heritage. We could also ask why Jehoiakim cut the scroll of Jeremiah and put it into the fire, or why the crowds and leaders united against Jesus.

What criterion is left? There is none. Denominations can judge who should be ordained. Individual churches can still make the choice of whom they will hear. Parties within the church can uphold the ancient creeds or the canon against the uses that are made of them. However, the grasp and presentation of the message is an exercise of the preacher's imagination, under the guidance of the Spirit of God. Ultimately, only God can separate true from false visions. This is not satisfying, since it leaves us without a clear and firm assurance. It is like submitting an examination paper, but not having it marked. However, this may be what it means to walk and preach and

program by faith. We do these things as seers who, as
Barth suggested, have the Bible in one hand and the
newspaper in the other, and keep open to the nudges of
the Spirit of God.

> A Hair perhaps divides the False and True.
> Yes; and a single Alif were the clue—
> Could you but find it—to the Treasure-house,
> And peradventure, to the Master too.
> —The Rubáiyát of Omar Khayyám,
> tr. by Edward FitzGerald

The important thing is to be obedient to the inner witness you feel, and hold it at all costs. That strange story
in I Kings 13 illustrates this point well. The story contains
the tensions between true and false prophecy, and the
difficulty of untangling them. The true prophet has delivered a message from God to Bethel, as he knew he was
to do. Then he returned to his home by another route,
as God told him to do. On the way, he was met by
another prophet, who coaxed him home for some rest and
relaxation, and the prophet knew that this he should not
do. The enticer said, "I also am a prophet as you are, and
an angel spoke to me by the word of the LORD, saying,
'Bring him back with you into your house that he may eat
bread and drink water.'" Observing these spotless credentials, the prophet went home with him, and ultimately met disaster. He had turned his back on his own
best insight in order to listen to someone else's insight.
H. H. Rowley makes the sage observation:

For the prophet who, in his own inner consciousness, has
known the certainty of the divine word, to defer to a word
received through any other, incompatible with it, is disobedience. He is substituting what *may* be of man for what he is
sure was of God.[32]

CHAPTER 4

SPEAKING FOR GOD TODAY

Is creativity so unique and specialized that no general patterns can be detected? Does one hang up one's mind like an Aeolian harp, waiting for a mysterious wind to blow? Or, are there some observable patterns—suggestions, if not laws—of creativity?

What have creative people found out about the process in which they are engaged? All of them rely on imagination. All struggle to bring half-formed intuitions out into the open. Does their experience help the minister, who must do the same thing on a weekly basis? Furthermore, does academic training help or hinder creativity? In this respect are creative people like Bing Crosby, who avoided singing lessons because he feared the loss of his style? Or are they highly trained in technical aspects, only bringing to their field that mysterious plus whereby knowledge advances?

What about idiosyncrasies in creative people? Are these quirks outside the creative process or vital to it? Or are they constant reminders that creative people are individuals who are not afraid to be themselves? This in itself would be a valuable lesson, the need to be uniquely yourself. These are some of the questions we raise as we examine the creative process for any help it can give the preacher.

Certainly, for the minister, more than intellect and formal training are needed, yet these are vital as background. We will assume for the moment that the would-be seer has had technical training. The subjects of science, English, history, psychology, economics, and the entire undergraduate round are essential. So are the superstructure subjects of the theological seminary: Bible, language, theology, church history, homiletics, Christian education, church administration, counseling. So, too, are the post-seminary disciplines of continuing education, continual reading, continuous pondering. Many times, talk of creativity short-circuits reference to years of preparation when the sky seems brass and the earth iron, and no inspiration lights up the mind. Therefore, let us assume that the standard preparation surrounds the seer. Let us grant, too, the truth of Wesley in his response to a woman who was critical of his scholarship. She knew he studied Greek and Hebrew, and she felt these were unnecessary, and told him so. "Mr. Wesley, God can get along right well without your scholarship." To this, he replied, "True, madam, and God can get along quite well without your ignorance." For our part, in a day of mass education, most seers have been through the schools rather than just off the fields of Tekoa. At least we will assume such a background. But what else is involved in being a seer?

The Willingness to Be Yourself

Of the essence is the willingness to be yourself, and to trust your inner formulation of things. We have already seen that ancient seers had no ready-made script. They were neither parrots of others' lines nor consummate actors of a classical script. They took the still more ancient revelation of what God had done and reworked it. When it came out again, it was fresh and in a new setting. What God had done became for their hearers the more relevant statement of what God was doing. Above all, they were themselves. If antagonists told them to peddle their products elsewhere, they stood firm. If a king took their words and pared them off in strips and threw them into the fire, they stubbornly wrote them over again. If, like Micaiah, they were thrown into prison for their vision, they awaited vindication. They demonstrated what it means to be oneself and to trust the inner monitor.

Even the Bible's lack of firm criteria is an encouragement to be oneself. There is no way to hold up a contemporary message alongside a Biblical passage so that there can be a point-by-point matching test. That would be a rerun and not a fresh statement, a case of wooden orthodoxy. No, seers are their own persons. They touch base with tradition so as to score on their own. They do not have the security of the ready-made. In a sense, seers are always in a posture of setting out not knowing where they are going, yet confident that the journey has some divine underpinnings. The first step in the process of seeing is: Be yourself, and trust yourself.

Of course, imitation helps. Science students rerun experiments that have long since been verified. Aspiring painters attend museums with sketchbooks. Copying is an essential step toward originality. D. H. Lawrence confesses that the greatest pleasure he ever got came from copying Fra Angelico's *Flight Into Egypt* and Carpaccio's *Death of Procris*.[33] Just so, the minister-seer in early stages must copy. He might take a text and imagine how a pulpit master would see it. He would be familiar with

Spurgeon's no-nonsense Scriptural outlines, and with Robertson's balanced two-point polarities, and with Fosdick's art of stabbing the attention awake with the theme stated clearly in the first or second paragraph, a theme as timely as the morning newspaper. He could learn the art of deft literary illustration from Arthur Gossip, and the human interest story from Weatherhead. Peter Marshall could show him how to dramatize a sermon, and Fred Speakman could instruct him on how to put the same thing into dialogue form.

All this need not bottle up creativity. Such copying will rather develop discernment and taste. However, the preacher cannot stop there, and certainly must not become a lifelong plagiarist. D. H. Lawrence, after paying tribute to the artists he copied, continued:

Then, suddenly, by having a blank canvas, I discovered I could make a picture myself. That is the point, to make a picture on a blank canvas. And I was 40 before I had the courage to try. Then, it became an orgy, making pictures.[34]

The problem for many is that they never get beyond the copying stage, and for many reasons. Sometimes, it is a cop-out on hard work. More often, it is a disillusionment with the importance of the work. A sermon, then, seems to be an organizational gimmick that has lasted long beyond its usefulness. Since the dying thing cannot yet be buried, the next best thing is to sermonize quickly. Copy, get it over with, get on to something more important. Grab a ready-made sheet from an opportunist press, and fill the twenty minutes. Use the preparation time for other things that matter. So, the sermon crepehangers spoil the effects of preaching by failing to demonstrate what real preaching is.

There is still another group who run from the responsibility of preaching their own insights. These stumble over their critical faculty and never reach confidence in speaking a word on their own. It is not that they shun hard work, or even that they have given up on the sermon's possibilities. However, though they are highly trained in using their minds, they are not highly trained in listening to their inner voices. Again, the result is copying rather than proclaiming. The poet Allen Tate refers to these as the university men and women of ages twenty to twenty-five whose imaginations have been stifled. "They've read all the criticism, they know all the answers, and they are so much aware of what has been accomplished by the two preceding generations, that they tend to be intimidated by it. Or, if they do write, they don't strike out much on their own."[35] Tate goes on to describe the problem as "a certain kind of ignorance of one's own time." It is certainly this, but also an ignorance of our own best insights as they are prodded by the interaction of Scripture and experience. At some point, we must leave the steadying hand of tradition and other people's thought, and be willing to walk on our own.

One night, in ancient Shiloh, a young boy was trying to sleep. He was a student at the religious center run by Eli the priest. Three times he heard a voice that called his name, and three times he checked things out with the patriarch headmaster. Finally, it dawned on both that God was trying to speak a new word through Samuel. The times were empty of visions. Ordinary affairs proceeded, but the politics of theocracy were corrupt. The appropriate word was *Ichabod,* for the glory had departed. In this situation, God gave a vision to Samuel. It was not a polite or pleasant message. The establishment was under judgment. Samuel was to be a spokesman of judgment. As with so many later seers, Samuel was to cross swords with the *status quo* and conventional piety. Eli said, "Do not hide from me what God has said." Samuel spoke, and in his speaking, "the Lord appeared again at Shiloh" (I Sam. 3:21).

The first lesson of seeing is to be yourself. Speak what you have heard. Many who have found new paths have had to brave the taunts of those who preferred the old and familiar. Whether like Elijah having to flee Israel or like Stravinsky having to flee the Paris concert hall after the premiere of *The Rite of Spring,* creators often create disturbance. That is why they need convictions and the courage to do a new thing. One artist, who was starting on the road to national prominence, was asked how she survived when so many critics had turned their backs on her work, and were only now starting to come around. "Oh," she said, "you survive by knowing that what you have produced is really you and not somebody else, and that you have done the painting as faithfully as you can with your present skill and experience." That could have been spoken by Degas, Monet, or Sisley, for the Impressionists were repeatedly ruled out of the national exhibits at the Salon; or it could have been echoed by Galileo, Kepler, or Harvey, whose discoveries contradicted the teaching of the church. We exist as preachers by the ability to reveal what is really inside, and what is really our own, despite the consequences.

Aspects of Being Yourself

We return to the original question. What is involved in seeing? Be yourself! But the answer has many aspects. On the one hand, one must have confidence as a minister that the Samuel experience is repeatable. That is, there must be the feeling that God's message arrives in a unique form to those who must proclaim it. In Samuel's case, the message implies direct communication. With Amos, the message is mediated by events and objects. Sometimes, as with Mozart, the finished piece is given with the initial reception; other times, as with Beethoven, it is developed in struggle through many revisions. Sometimes the pivot of energy is felt to be outside ourselves. Intellectual workers such as Spenser, Nietzsche, William Rowan Hamilton, and C. F. Gauss, and artists such as Shelley, Blake, Max Ernst, and Henry James, all testify to such an automatic take-over. Others feel the pivot of energy is in themselves. They are more conscious of working out laboriously their own insights. Anton Chekhov has insisted that only a lunatic would create automatically:

To deny that artistic creation involves problems and purposes would be to admit that an artist creates without premeditation, without design, under a spell. Therefore, if an artist boasted to me of having written a story without previously settled design, but by inspiration, I should call him a lunatic.[36]

However, whether the effort to speak the new word seems to originate with more "take-over" from God, or more "take charge" by the intellect, the result is the same. To be yourself as a preacher means that you believe you have something to say from God that is uniquely yours.

Another aspect of being yourself in the creative process is in accepting the wide range of idiosyncrasies, and in not being intimidated by those which are not your own. When Fosdick preached, he had a habit of pacing and removing his handkerchief from time to time. Many students started pacing and mopping in sympathetic vibration, but the actions did not fit them as they did Fosdick. In a similar way, other giants have found comfort in peculiar mannerisms or customs that were not meant to be copied so much as observed. To make these idiosyncrasies the norm is to find substance in the ephemeral. Yet, since these surrounding phenomena of creativity are always present in some form, they give freedom for the new seers to be themselves with their own set of idiosyncrasies.

For instance, every preacher probably has one time when the creative juices flow more freely than at other times. All aspiring preachers should find that period in which they do their best work and take advantage of it. Aaron Copland never writes much during the commotion of the day. When things settle down, after 10 P.M., his ideas flow. He remembered someone who said that most intimate letters are written after 10 P.M., and since music is an intimate experience, with feeling being put into sound, it is fitting to him that this is the time for composing. Yet Copland tells of his friend Henry Schuman, who must get everything written before 10 A.M. or he accomplishes nothing.[37] A. E. Housman confides that his inspirations come after lunch, and usually when he has finished a pint of beer and gone out for a walk of two or three hours. Arthur Koestler finds that midafternoon until early evening is his best time. If he writes three hundred words, and they seem to hang together, he is pleased and can relax with a cocktail.

Repeatedly, those who talk about their inspiration claim that they work at their appointed times whether they feel particularly inspired or not. Often the appointment with desk and pad provokes the insight rather than the inrush of an idea provoking the writing. Another matter of general agreement is that the period when one is just coming out of sleep is particularly productive. Normal interference is down. Mental associations spring together, usually when the person has thought about the subject before going to sleep. Some writers keep a pad by the bed so they are ready for the expected visitation. Yet the patterns vary widely. For most, there is one time that is better than others. To find this, and to be yourself without mimicry, is part of the creative process.

Length of time needed to create varies, and the "normal" does not exist, either to guide or to intimidate. Peter Drucker makes the helpful suggestion that we operate best when we reserve long blocks of time for planning, at least two hours per sitting.[38] This allows for brooding time and all the extraneous motions that are akin to the restlessness of cats before they settle down. Brooding time is not recognized as valuable by activists. It seems like wasted time, in which one is doing nothing but staring or pacing or fingering pencils. In reality, it is often the threshold of creating. It is the paradox of doing nothing so as to do something. It is the time to let haphazard excitements settle, and to focus on the still small voice. In some two-hour periods, the ideas start to flow pell-mell. Interruption by phone or visitor could prevent ideas from coming into consciousness and out on paper.

The classic case of someone who interrupted a magnificent vision is the "man from Porlock." Coleridge was staying in a lonely farmhouse between Porlock and Linton in the summer of 1797. A flood of images came to his mind, an entire poem's worth, which he raced to set down, his famous *Kubla Khan.* While he was thus occupied, a man from Porlock knocked, and discussed business that detained Coleridge for an hour. When he went back to his work, the recollection of his train of thought had vanished and would not return.[39] Blocks of time, long blocks of uninterrupted time, are needed. But not needed by everyone on every occasion. An Abraham Lincoln can write a Gettysburg Address on an envelope while riding a train. Paul can preach a fine sermon with only the preparation time it takes to walk the road to Mars' Hill. Sometimes while reading something entirely extraneous, the mind makes several shuttle stops in and out of next Sunday's topic, often delivering important points that only need a minor polishing. Again, no single time plan is possible. The only advice is the familiar: Be yourself. Don't be intimidated by someone else's method.

One strange stimulus to creativity involves sensory cues. These seem bizarre, and were it not that they keep popping up as devices of great thinkers, they might easily be passed over. Knowlson in 1917 collected examples of cues that various thinkers seemed to need to have within perceptual range.[40] Dr. Johnson needed to have a purring cat, orange peel, and plenty of tea to drink. Balzac wrote all night, stimulated by constant cups of very strong black coffee. Zola pulled down the blinds at midday because he found more stimulus for his thought in artificial light. Carlyle was forever trying to construct a soundproof room, while Proust achieved one. Schiller seems to have depended on the smell of decomposing apples, which he habitually kept in his desk. Kipling reported his inability to write creatively with a lead pencil; his strongly autonomous thought processes seemed to demand the blackest ink, all blue-blacks being "an abomination" to his creative tendencies. Stephen Spender depended on coffee and tobacco while composing verse, while W. H. Auden was addicted to tea. Perhaps, as Spender argues, these supposed eccentricities are "due to mechanical habits or rituals developed in order to concentrate."[41] The fact remains that they are numerous, necessary, and varied enough that no thinker should try to eliminate his, nor conform to the pattern of someone else.

But these instances—how to schedule time, how long a time, concentration devices—are extraneous to the message itself. We assume as preachers that God has some message to be spoken through us, and that this message will come even though we must wait for it. We also assume that the message develops as a creative insight which requires the courage to claim it in its uniqueness. "Be yourself" certainly means be faithful to your own message, not to one read over someone else's shoulder. The thrust of the message, as well as the need for honesty in the face of variety, is apparent.

Variety in Receiving the Message

There is no evidence that when Luke wrote his Gospel he received the message out of the blue or with dramatic suddenness. Quite the reverse. He claims in the prologue that he went on a manuscript hunt. He may have interviewed eyewitnesses, checked into evidence, listened to Paul. But primarily he checked manuscripts and tried to arrange the events in the life of Christ in an orderly way.

Paul received his message in a different way. He entered the Christian faith by a sudden and life-changing mystic vision. He immediately spent three years in a desert, where he conferred with no one. His venture into Europe began with a vision of a Macedonian man, and a call for help. He spoke of being caught up to the third heaven, and seeing things past description. These two men, Luke and Paul, boon companions in their ministry, were as different as day and night in their manner of receiving the message. And each was self-assured enough to state his method and his differences.

Methodical differences no doubt color the message. Those who see as Paul saw may have more nerve and certainty, more hard-driving conviction. The analysts, like Luke, are more cautious and subdued. They must piece things together, make deductions, consult the bottom line. One seer has charisma, while the other has solidity. One, like Luther, paints in broad strokes; the other, like Melanchthon, etches the fine points. For either one to be like the other would be as impossible as for David to wear Saul's armor. They both must be themselves, and they are both useful insofar as they remain themselves.

Unfortunately, the Pauline method of seeing is often the stereotype of all seeing, and the longed-for ideal where it is absent. We mistakenly believe that inspired geniuses must work by momentary insight rather than slow, methodical scarch. Isaiah's vision in the Temple and Peter's discovery at Joppa seem more Godlike than forty days in the wilderness or a few years working with manuscripts. We sometimes feel that what is "out of the blue" must be authentic and that what is searched and pondered must raise some doubts. But this is nonsense. Some of the greatest insights have come from a step-by-step search.

Two examples must suffice. Van Gogh, in a letter to a friend, describes the over-and-over-again quality of his work.

When I have a model who is quiet and steady, and with whom I am acquainted, then I draw repeatedly till there is one drawing that is different from the rest, which does not look like an ordinary study, but more typical and with more feeling. . . . As to *The Little Winter Gardens,* for example, you said yourself they had so much feeling; all right, but that was not accidental—I drew them several times and there was no feeling in them. Then afterwards—after I had done the ones that were so stiff—came the others.[42]

If it were possible by method to go directly to the drawing that is the right one, who would spend the anguish of all the intermediary steps? That would be akin to visions in the third heaven, where the brush or the tongue or the pen obeys the vision. For Van Gogh, there was no such immediacy, despite the appearance of sudden insight. Instead, there had to be drawing upon drawing, until the secret was unlocked and the message delivered.

The same methodical plodding would characterize Beethoven. To the uninitiated, his works seem sublime. Unless the background is searched out, it may look as though one day Beethoven was dazzled with great themes, which he had simply to set down quickly. Not so. It is instructive to many and disappointing to some, to see the genius working through numerous revisions. His works did not spring fully armed like Minerva out of Jupiter's head. Paul Hindemith describes many of Beethoven's works going through five or more intermediate steps from the first structural treatment to the final version.[43] Hindemith also notes that some of the first versions are in quality so far below the final form that we should be inclined to attribute them to some undistinguished composer. Yet Beethoven must plod through the many stages of development, chiseling and molding desperately in order to produce a convincing form.

The Van Goghs and the Beethovens have their counterparts in preachers whose wastebaskets are full of the foolscap of false starts and ideas that are not quite together. To get the right word instead of the almost right word, to make an outline so that each part connects with the central theme, to find the illustration that throws light on the topic without upstaging the other points, to hit upon the word order that has cadence and pause, to know when to end the sermon without redundancy, this process is tedious for most. Such workers compose line upon line, precept upon precept, hour by hour, like Luke at a desk with a Gospel to write and a hundred scraps of parchment lying around. This method seems at times so uninspiring as to be apart from grace. Yet plodders have insight too, if they are willing to be themselves and accept a plodder's creativity. And, not to be overlooked, the method is often built into the message.

This last fact needs examining for the encouragement it gives to plodders. If Mozart and Beethoven, for instance, had both ended with music that had the same musical impact, but reached that end by different routes, then the shorter route would have been the better. If a resort can be reached either by a turnpike or by a longer two-lane road through nondescript towns, only a masochist would choose the long, circuitous road. The fallacy here, as applied to music or to preaching, is in the assumption that the end result is the same despite the route taken. This is not true. Mozart and Beethoven were both geniuses, but their music is as different as their method. Mozart's music is clean, bright, crisp, and precise. It is classical, uplifting, fit for the ballroom and the dance. Beethoven's music is romantic, strong, passionate, rich. His music has marks of the suffering of the composer who must rise from the depths. The struggle is evident, the joy-in-pain aspect. Whether this kind of insight is possible by easy transmission is debatable. Perhaps only those who struggle for the vision can capture the struggle in the finished product. The rejection of Jeremiah, his desire to flee, his wish never to have been born, are aspects of what he sees and records. So it is with all those who record faithfully from their pain.

Getting Your Own Message

But what of the message itself? In the message the real need arises to be yourself, and to work through only that which is honestly yours. It is possible to accept idiosyncrasies in work habits and method and to develop a pattern that is personal and workable, while failing to bring to light what one's hands have handled and one's eyes have seen. A scissors-and-paste sermon may take time, and may deceive even the elect into thinking that a creation has happened, when actually it is only a collage of other people's thought. If positive thinking is in vogue, then a few pieces from Peale or Schuller will do. If the theme is patriotism, then baptize the Founding Fathers and use a few quotes from the diary of John Adams. In no time at all, ministers called to be seers become hack writers crying "Peace, peace," when there is no peace.

There are at least two dangers in failing to come to terms with your own message. On the one hand, you can project ideas and feelings that are true for someone else but not for you. These lack the authenticity of your personality. Since preaching is still, in Phillips Brooks's famous phrase, truth communicated through personality, such a falseness is disastrous. On the other hand, a message that is not truly yours may cater to what the audience wants rather than to what you sense is God's message.

The latter danger is not simply preaching to pacify rather than to judge. It is not, to use the Old Testament motif, preaching weal when God wants woe. Perhaps in the Old Testament, false prophets were more apt to speak in glowing terms about the future, and not to point out the thunderheads, and the dry wadis that could funnel a torrent of floodwaters. But the mere preaching of gloom and judgment is not necessarily a mark of true preaching. Flip the dial on any Sunday morning in America, and the radio thunders with the sonorous voices of hellfire evangelists. They know who Gog and Magog are, and where the battle of Armageddon will be fought, and what newspaper headlines clue in to what Bible passages. However, just as "everybody talkin' 'bout heaven ain't goin' there," everybody preaching a gloomy jeremiad has not necessarily stood by the burning bush. The radio preachers that fit this description usually have phrases and outlines and conclusions that are as predictable as soap powder commercials. Their fault is not just that they give the audience what it wants (and let's admit that a large radio audience delights to hear a message of doom), or that they stand on the opposite shore and throw stones. Their fault, among others, is that they are just plain dull.

Messages that do not spring from the viscera are apt to be dull. They take popular ideas and repeat them. Whether of heaven or hell, the messages do not break new ground. They are "safe" even if they deal with Armageddon. The audience loves to hear that old story. They will judge the orthodoxy by the familiar sounds. That is the danger of neglecting your inner vision. Visions break new ground. They relate old material, the story of Jesus and his love, but with a different accent, and directed to new problems. The new accent calls for new thought and gives the congregation a new challenge. The sermon is not looking back to an exodus story that has been repeated from childhood. Instead, the sermon reminds the congregation that it is also on the exodus, with Amalek up ahead, and no certainty that manna will come in the morning, or that water will flow at Meribah. Through the message of insight, the preacher stands with his congregation at the border of a new Promised Land whose outline is only partly visible, but whose walled cities and giants have grown to enormous proportions. This message is positioned in the middle of a new wilderness, a land of risk and peril, with nothing to rely on but faith in the faithful God, and the promise of a cloud no bigger than a man's hand, off in the distance.

Any message that fails to come to terms with the uniqueness inside will fail because it is either too dull or too safe. Aaron Copland comments on this problem in many modern musical programs. The audience have become accustomed to the romantic sounds of Brahms and Tchaikovsky. They expect them, and applaud. The newer music sounds raucous by comparison and the rhythms unfamiliar. New instruments, not "proper" for the symphony orchestra, are featured, and the melody line is not as important. The new music needs a hearing, says Copland. It will be the familiar sound of the next generation. But the conductor, despite his personal bias, must hold back on too much that is new, because the paying public will not tolerate it. "No one after drinking old wine desires new; for he says, 'the old is good' " (Luke 5:39). As a result, concludes Copland, we stick to what is safe, and music halls are turned into museums.[44] By our sticking to sounds they accept, the audience gradually lose all need to exercise freely a musical judgment, which is needed if music is to be a developing art.

This discussion about music halls carries over directly into the sanctuary. That is where old wine is popular. Old themes, old songs, old interpretations. A "liberal" church will have a Rauschenbusch flavor; a "conservative" church may have a Moody zeal. Both lose their way in dullness, because nothing creative is happening. To create is to make something new. For the preacher, to create is to sing a new song, which may come out free of old

labels, and with a slightly jarring new rhythm. This newness is what disturbed the Judaism of the New Testament, which heard familiar Scripture with a different
twist. The newness also disturbed Christian society in
1517, when Luther saw an old Scripture in a new way.
Barth performed the same function in the midst of the
bland liberalism of the 1920's, and Bonhoeffer from
prison shot new themes into the deadness of the post-
Protestant era. The newness was a response to the same
drummer who was giving a different beat, measured and
far away on the future of their time. These men did not
wait for accolades or external sanctions. The lion roared,
and they heard, even though most of their contemporaries did not.

However, there is an interesting problem that all authentic prophets face. Suppose what you say is not consistent with what you have said on previous occasions?
That is, suppose Richard Neuhaus and William Sloane
Coffin sound the bell of social activism in the '60s and
then beat the drum for a more conventional piety in the
'70s? Is one of those positions wrong, or are these men
hypocritical? From the Selma marches to the Hartford
Affirmation seems a long distance to travel within ten
years.[45] The same might be said of Paul van Buren's
old-style secular theology and new-style metaphysics, or
the still earlier van Buren who was a staunch advocate of
Karl Barth. Should we say, with tongue in cheek, "Will
the real van Buren please stand up?" Or should we say,
along with Martin Marty, that Cox and Coffin have a
keen awareness of public opinion, and made their shifts
simply to capture the news media after several years of
religious ennui?[46] These judgments seem too harsh. They
make the people mentioned seem like opportunists and
allow no freedom for the shifting nature of religious imag-

ination. Sometimes consistency is a difficult if not impossible ideal for the preacher to achieve.

Creative thinkers often testify that when they are seized by an inspiration they are never sure just where things will come out at the end. Granted, there is some consistency. Beethoven does not write poems. Poincaré does not paint masterpieces. But, granting the obvious, creativity is breaking new ground that is not always known to the seer at the moment. There is in the act of creating no straitjacket of consistency that is operating. Artists, preachers, writers, and seers leave others to fit what they are doing into appropriate categories, for they are still finding their way down roads they have not traveled before. They must, as Robert Penn Warren reiterates, discover the possibilities of the germ they start with, and they only know what they really mean after they create it.[47] The feeling is conveyed that seers in all fields work at a white-hot intensity with ideas not always subject to the cold analysis of reason or logic. Their fault is more apt to be a too-high enthusiasm rather than hypocrisy or dishonesty.

Another special factor of religious vision that makes consistency difficult is the nature of the thing seen. The intuitions involve Scripture, personal experience, and historical times. All three of these are shifting; so much so, that to paraphrase Heraclitus, you can't step into the same vision twice. Knowledge of Scripture is constantly expanding. The personal growth of the seer is likewise expanding. Even if his or her knowledge did not increase an iota, the aging process gives a constantly shifting perspective. The seer then stands on a constantly moving platform.

And then, the times through which we pass never hold still to get a once-and-for-all accurate reading. If you ask preachers, "What do you see?" they might respond: "When?" "Under what circumstances?" "With what information at my disposal?" "I cannot give you a clear answer that is not subject to change, for times have changed." Religious vision must take place when everything nailed down is coming loose. To expect consistency of the sort that might be appropriate for math or logic is a bit unreal. It is only appropriate, however, to expect the seer to be himself and honest with his intuitions at the particular moment of working them out. Once again, the refrain is: Be yourself.

Along with this Heraclitean observation, that consistency is difficult because of too many shifting parts, there is the depth dimension of seeing. We are not simply in the realm of ideas. We are positioned somewhere between heaven and earth, with the difficult assignment of trying to look both ways on behalf of others who want to see but can't. Despite revelation, nothing is totally clear in that nebulous borderland. It is a totally false assumption that what comes from God is clear and arrow-straight, or that modern prophets receive a message resembling an unbending shaft of light. With God there is no variableness, neither shadow of turning, but there certainly is variableness in the receiver. In the pregnant words of John Baillie, "It takes two to make a revelation." Therefore we must allow for variation in the message. We see through a glass darkly. A message given at one time is apt to sound different in another time. It may even sound contradictory. All we can ask of the seer is faithfulness rather than consistency.

The problem of consistency is not addressable only to modern seers. It could be raised within the canon. Did Jeremiah approve of Josiah's reform or didn't he? Did Amos proclaim only a message of God's stern judgment, or did he add a shaft of hope in his closing moments? Did Jesus say, "He who is not with me is against me," and did he not also say, "He that is not against us is for us"? Did Paul really believe the Second Coming was around the corner, as in I Thessalonians, or did he sense it was yet a way off, as in II Thessalonians? Was the belief in the Second Coming of utmost urgency, as in both Thessalonian letters, or was it subordinate to other teaching, as in the Corinthian letters? It is better not to make a fetish of consistency, particularly when men and women are in the first flush of insight. In the happy phrase of the anthropologist R. R. Marrett, "religion is danced out before it is thought out."

This does not disparage the need for consistency, nor the demand of logical minds that it must be found. However, it is to suggest that consistency is twice removed from creative insight and is never the first criterion of those who see. Consistency belongs in the natural sciences, where controlled, repeatable experiments can be conducted. It belongs to law, where old categories and precedents are sought which apply to the new. It belongs to philosophy, where new knowledge is deduced or induced from the known. However, even in these fields, a truly creative person breaks up the old consistencies, necessitating a new scholasticism. When Einstein invades Newtonian physics, or Edward Coke or Oliver Wendell Holmes rethinks law, or Heidegger rethinks philosophy, all the old consistencies fall apart, and a new synthesis is demanded.

The same is true of religion. Systematic theology aims at consistency, but interestingly enough, it can never build a complete fence around the subject it handles. It must wait for primary insights before it can codify the results. It waits for the dance to be over, so to speak. But when it gets to work and writes the last page, some new dance begins. The work of codification must begin again. Thus, when Luther and Calvin have danced out their primary visions, and when the scholastics of the next century have put the dogma into consistent creeds, a Schleiermacher comes along to make the old formulations no longer adequate. To worry about consistency is first of all to stand once removed from religious vision, and it is to forget that the vision is needed as the raw material from which systematizers manufacture their creeds. Creeds crumble as new visions supersede old ones. The creeds are not eternal canons to measure what prophets see.

This, in part, explains the shift in Coffin and Neuhaus from the '60s to the '70s, from Selma to Hartford, from an affirmation of social action as primary to an affirmation of the supernatural. They may be en route to a new position that breaks up for many of their followers, as well as for themselves, their old consistent pattern. But who is to say? Who can really tell if the new insight is momentous, or an aberration that needs correcting?

Certainly, at the moment of putting forth a new position, every creator feels right. Creators are caught up in enthusiasm. They literally explode with the new charge. This is a valid mark of the creative process. Picasso once affirmed to Christian Zervos, "The essential in these times of moral misery is to create enthusiasm."[48] And again, "The artist is a receptacle of emotions come from no matter where; from the sky, the earth, a piece of paper, a passing figure, a cobweb."[49] All contact with the new has excitement that runs the gamut from pathos to ecstasy. In this one aspect, enthusiasm, the creators are usually marked off from the systematizers. Truth has high feeling for the seers of truth, and it also excites the hearers. They are apt to say, "Did not our hearts burn within us?" and even give the impression that they have been affected by new wine.

Yet enthusiasm is also the mark of deviation. False prophets also could dance before the Lord. The new excites even where the new is false. Therefore, who is to say whether what is seen is a new and valuable shoot from the stem of the old? It is often impossible to judge at the time the new is put forth. That judgment awaits the passage of time, the judgment of the systematizers who are far enough removed from the message to be objective, and the wisdom of Gamaliel. It was the old Rabbi Gamaliel who spoke to the Sanhedrin about the totally new message of Jesus' resurrection, so shattering to mainline Judaism. Gamaliel advised: "If this plan . . . is of men, it will fail; but if it is of God, you will not be able to overthrow them. You might even be found opposing God!" (Acts 5:38–39). Therefore, consistency should be no fetish for those who dream dreams. Consistency looks backward, creativity looks ahead into the unknown.

Yet there is one attribute of seers that functions like an external censor. It is the critical side of personality, which teams up with the creative side. This attribute does not have the passion of the creative drive. It is slightly detached from the immediate creation. It is the gadfly; the daemon of honesty. At the same time that a creation is taking place and the imagination is churning toward something new, a more objective side of personality is looking on, raising questions, driving toward authenticity. It is almost as if two interior parts of personality were in constant dialogue, one forging ahead with high zeal, the other standing with arms folded and criticizing what is happening. Or to change the figure, it is as if the creative thrust were seated under the white light of a police barracks, while the critical half drove home relentless questions, all in the interest of absolute truth. "Look here, is what you're creating really you?" "Does it say what you intended?" "Have you eliminated the extraneous so that the essential stands out?" And, in the case of preachers: "Are you honest with the text?" "Did the passage really mean that?" "Did you phrase it precisely with the right words?" "Is it really gospel or is it editorial analysis?" "Is the sermon what you really feel, or just what you think the congregation expects you to feel?"

Creative people deal with this ruthless censor differently. Aaron Copland holds it in check so that the creative urge does not get scared and run away. He writes: "The inspired moment may sometimes be described as a kind of hallucinatory state of mind: one half of the personality emotes and dictates while the other half listens and takes note. The half that listens had better look the other way, had better simulate a half attention only, for the half that dictates is easily disgruntled, and avenges itself for too close inspection by fading away entirely."[50] Yet others realize that the inspector daemon is beneficent. Without its work, we might settle for what is second best. We might miss entirely the many-splendored thing. The painter Ben Shahn describes his own development in art as follows:

During the early French-influenced part of my artistic career, I painted landscapes in a Post-Impressionist vein, pleasantly peopled with bathers, or I painted nudes, or studies of my friends. The work had a nice professional look about it, and it rested, I think, on a fairly solid academic training. It was during those years that the inner critic first began to play hara-kiri with my insides. With such ironic words as, "It has a nice professional look about it," my inward demon was prone to ridicule or tear down my work in just those terms in which I was wont to admire it. The questions, "Is that enough?" "Is that all?" began to plague me. Or, "This may be art, but is it my own art?" And then, I began to realize that however professional my work might appear, even however original it might be, it still did not contain the central person which, for good or ill, was myself.[51]

These questions of ruthless honesty are not those of the twice-removed systematizer. They impinge on the insides of the creative person in the act of creating. They are far more than questions of congregation or critic, and for that reason they can be totally filtered out. Yet to give them a hearing is essential to true creativity of any sort, especially the creation of the sermon. In secular language, the process is for the self to help you be yourself, which is the only possible existence that is authentic and satisfying. In theological language, the process is for you to shape what was originally inspired so that the end product, the sermon, conforms to the will of God. This also makes for authenticity and satisfaction.

However, what if two claim to be seers, but come up with diametrically opposite answers? Think of Billy Graham as compared to Harvey Cox, or both in relation to the late Reinhold Niebuhr; Norman Vincent Peale compared to Edmund Steimle; Hans Küng over against Cardinal Ottaviani. Who is the true prophet and who the false? Shall Gamaliel be called on again for his wisdom? Will the test of time reveal the one who speaks for God? As we indicated in the preceding chapter, there are really no adequate tests to fully disclose the true message. The so-called test of time might reveal that one message endured longer than the other, that it had more adherents, that it triggered other thinkers. But these and similar criteria are all external to the creative process, which is a distinctively internal, self-authenticating experience.

Better to realize that the truth of God is many-sided, complex, within and beyond our comprehension. As the ancient Symmachus put it, "It is impossible that so great a mystery should be approached by one road only." This suggests infinite diversity in the messages that are received from different seers, even though they live with the same Scriptures and in the same historical time. All could be authentic and none should feel intimidated by the other, and each should have the courage to be himself or herself.

Paul Hindemith has a useful analogy in speaking about musical inspiration. He feels that everybody has musical inspiration, not just composers. We are all touched by "a vague curve of sound."[52] The difference between a composer and the rest of us is that in the laypeople's minds, these inspirations die away unused in their earliest infancy. The creative musician knows how to catch them and subject them to further treatment. But then, Hindemith asks the further question as to why some composers end up with hackwork whereas a Beethoven works laboriously through revisions until he reaches the final form to which the first "nudge" was pointing. He explains it in terms of musical vision, which Beethoven has, and others do not.[53] It is, says Hindemith, like a flash of lightning in the night. Within a second of time, we see a broad landscape not only in its general outlines, but with every detail. Although we could never describe each single component of the picture, we feel that not even the smallest blade of grass escapes our attention. We experience a view immensely comprehensive and at the same time immensely detailed, a view that we could never have under normal daylight conditions, and perhaps not during the night either, if our senses and nerves were not strained by the extraordinary suddenness of the event.

Just so, says Hindemith, the authentic composer sees as if by a flash of lightning a complete musical form, both the whole and the relationship of the parts to the whole. Others who lack this vision may grind out pieces and glue each to each, but without the inner integrity of a comprehensive whole.

Hindemith's analogy of lightning applies to preachers as well as composers. The possibility exists for two contrary messages to be true, either because the two were standing back to back when the lightning flashed, or because they were in different parts of the terrain. If Amos sees a basket of summer fruit and prophesies doom, while his contemporary Hosea sees his love hold fast throughout a marital crisis and predicts mercy, we do not ask which one is speaking truly for God. We recognize the mystery of God, the night of our world, and the possibility that the lightning illuminates different parts of the landscape.

Incubating the Message

Can the lightning be encouraged, or is it totally unexpected? If the latter, how is preaching possible when it must be done every week on schedule, even when there are no storms? One answer is to begin early. Begin early in the week on an individual sermon. Begin early in the year on a general plan. Begin early, perhaps years early, with nonscheduled sermons, making use of notebook files for pregnant sentences, observations, possible outlines, illustrations. The reason is to permit time for the incubation of ideas, and particularly for productivity during nonwork times.

That incubation time is needed appeals to common sense, and therefore needs no great endorsement. Just to cite a few testimonies: Nietzsche describes in *Ecce Homo* how the ideas for his earlier book *Thus Spake Zarathustra* came to him on a specific occasion in the woods behind Lake Silvaplana in 1881. But he writes that "the period of gestation was 18 months before its sudden birth in February, 1883." Amy Lowell, writing of the processes involved in the composition of her poetry, refers to one instance when she dropped her subject into the unconscious very much as one drops a letter into a mailbox. Six months later, the poem was "there." Robert Louis Stevenson thus described his own methods in imaginative work: "Unconscious thought, there is the only method: macerate your subject, let it boil slow, then take the lid off and look in—and there your stuff is, good or bad."[54]

Such testimony indicates that Saturday night sermonizing is bound to be a frustrating experience. The incubation period is too short. The productive force of the unconscious mind is ignored. The "biological" growth of an idea is not often cut short by an "out of the blue" inspiration. Perhaps this is the partial truth behind Moses' trip to the desert, Elijah's flight to Horeb, Jesus' forty days in the wilderness, Paul's three years in the desert, Habakkuk's long stand on the watchtower. The vision tarries, and you must wait for it. Fortunately, lectionaries and the rhythm of the church year help in advance planning, though even with these, the eleventh commandment for creative preaching still comes down from the mount: Begin early!

Another factor, already alluded to, in the creative process is the uncanny way that insight comes while one is doing nothing, provided that hard work has first been put into the theme at hand. The advice seems to be to work hard and then walk away. Experience the frustrations of a subject that won't work itself into form, and then do nothing. With no guarantees, and with no compulsion to produce, production comes. The mathematician Henri Poincaré gave one of the classic descriptions of this phenomenon:

> For 15 days I strove to prove that there could not be any functions like those I have since called Fuchsian functions. I was then very ignorant. Every day I seated myself at my work table, stayed an hour or two, tried a great number of combinations and reached no results. One evening, contrary to my custom, I drank black coffee and could not sleep. Ideas arose in crowds; I felt them collide until pairs interlocked, so to speak, making a stable combination. By the next morning, I had established the existence of a class of Fuchsian functions. . . . I had only to write out the results.

Then, Poincaré made a further mathematical discovery, in an entirely unlooked-for way:

> Just at this time, I left Caen, where I was then living, to go on a geological excursion. The changes of travel made me forget my mathematical work. Having reached Coutances, we entered an omnibus to go some place or other. At the moment when I put my foot on the step, the idea came to me, without anything in my former thoughts seeming to have paved the way for it, that the transformations I had used to define the Fuchsian functions were identical with those of non-Euclidean geometry. I did not verify the idea; I should not have had time as, upon taking my seat in the omnibus, I went on with a conversation already commenced, but I felt a perfect certainty. On my return to Caen, for conscience' sake, I verified the result at my leisure.[55]

Poincaré's experience is not peculiar to mathematics, it is peculiar to creativity in general. Rollo May had a similar experience, equally dramatic, of an answer to a research problem that came when he had left his office and was "about 50 feet away from the entrance to the Eighth Street Station." May formulates a few rules of creativity. Among the rules are: hard work on the topic *prior to the breakthrough;* a rest, in which the "unconscious work" has been given a chance to proceed on its own, and after which the breakthrough may occur; the necessity of alternating work and relaxation, with the insight often coming at the moment of the break between the two, or at least within the break.[56] This insight, however, is not original with May. As far back as 1917, the psychologist T. S. Knowlson expressed the same as a "law governing one of the primary conditions essential for the occurrence of inspirations and insights: a period of close inquiry and reflection should be followed either by a change of subject or a period of inactivity."[57] But even before this analysis, hints of productive inactivity were buried in the wisdom of the East, as for example in the Zen lines:

> Sitting quietly, doing nothing,
> Spring comes. The grass grows by itself.

Several reactions to this insight stand out. First of all, every preacher can think of experiences where insight came while one was hoeing the garden or hammering a nail, after prolonged and futile effort. The problem is that these times are thought of as exceptional or weird, rather than what could be normal sources of creativity. Yet, to ponder and then to walk away and seem to do nothing takes time. The process assumes the time for alternation from work to relaxation and back to work again. But, finally, the ability to walk away is one of the hardest lessons for our work-oriented profession to learn. We are accustomed to keeping up a feverish pace, even priding ourselves on the stamina to keep at it. To sit and do nothing, to break for relaxation, to look away from a subject, takes discipline and an even greater act of will than keeping at it. Hutchinson calls it "masterful idleness" and claims that the cessation of effort for a time can make us neurotic. We are ashamed to be seen doing nothing.[58] In a similar vein, Robert Penn Warren writes: "Just the willingness to waste time, to know that you have to waste a lot of time and take responsibility for wasting the time. That's part of the discipline. And know that most days are going to be bad days. Just that: that you have to throw them away. The problem is to stay away from writing, not to get at it."[59] The advice comes from all sectors of the creative world: Go forward by seeming to stand still. This takes effort—a disciplined nonchalance and the time for alternation. Once again, begin early.

There is a final element in the process of creativity which has a strange New Testament sound. Creative people are childlike. This has been noted by several investigators in recent years. Abraham Maslow observed: "Self-actualizing creativeness was in many respects like the creativeness of all happy and secure children. It was spontaneous, effortless, innocent, easy, a kind of freedom from stereotypes and clichés. . . . Almost any child can perceive more freely, without *a priori* expectations about what ought to be there or what must be there or what has always been there. . . . They [my subjects] had a 'second naïveté,' as Santayana called it."[60]

In much the same way, Carl Rogers speaks of creative people as being open to experience.[61] By this he means they have a lack of rigidity, the ability to receive conflicting information without forcing closure upon the situation, and the ability to toy with elements and concepts. According to Rogers, they play spontaneously with ideas, colors, shapes, relationships—to juggle elements into impossible juxtapositions, to shape wild hypotheses, to make the given problematic, to express the ridiculous, to translate from one form to another, to transform into improbable equivalents. It is from this spontaneous toying and exploration that there arises the hunch, the creative seeing of life in a new and significant way.[62]

The capacity to toy with all of experience, as a child of endless curiosity, is a prerequisite for all seers, especially preachers. It was this ability that made Moses investigate a burning bush, or Elijah detect a cloud far out at sea, no bigger than a man's hand, or Jesus note a woman dropping an insignificant sum into the Temple treasury, or Paul pick up the significance of an altar to an unknown god. They detect the significance of the insignificant, and take time to explore it, and wonder. They have not been pressed into the mold of what everyone else thinks, or what is the acceptable convention. They are not afraid to be laughed at or ridiculed as they exclaim, "Look at that!" or as they ask the question, "Why?"

The problem with children's wonder and awe is that it so quickly gets dampened by adult expectancy. By scoldings and silent pressure, we enforce the expected, and native curiosity is destroyed. We do this to creative people too. Believers are derided as "Christians" in Antioch, just as some painters were nicknamed "Impressionists" in Paris, all with the intent of making light of something new on the horizon. Modern preachers have the same pressures placed upon them, which—if they succumb—will rob them of creativity. The scholastic tradition learned in seminary suggests conformity to what has been thought or done in the past. Denominational or particular church traditions pressure preachers to conform to current policies and expectations. The American tradition expects a large dose of patriotism and civil religion. The latest fad woos us from our own originality with a suggestion to jump on some bandwagon before it is too late. Meanwhile, the words of Jesus take on special significance. "Unless you turn and become like children, you will never enter the kingdom of heaven." To return to a second naïveté, to see the entire world shot through with the divine, to wonder and investigate, to keep open and range widely, this too is to be yourself, and to be a child who has some insights into the Kingdom.

CHAPTER 5

RECOVERING THE POWER TO SEE

When ministers prepare for the pulpit they often feel a certain uneasiness. Is what they are doing important anymore? Those who remember the past know inwardly that they can never recover the glory of those former days. The masters of the pulpit in past generations were "princes," and their followers were full of respect. Preachers in former days had an effect on politics and education, and gave sought-after opinions on current events. Theodore Parker, Wendell Phillips, Henry Ward Beecher, Washington Gladden, Horace Bushnell, Phillips Brooks, Henry Sloane Coffin, Ralph Sockman, Peter Marshall, Harry Emerson Fosdick. There were giants in the land in those days.

By contrast, preachers today feel that greatness has passed them by. They seem to wear cutaway coats in a day of leisure suits, and they know they are no longer in style. The action now is in science or social work. The teaching power of lectures or sermons is felt to be trivial. The transforming power of the faith obviously is not tied to preaching. The mood of America is not merely against the pulpit, but against church organization and procedure in general. Young people follow new "princes," many of whom fly in from the Orient. Life seems to go on acceptably, even without regular church attendance. No wonder the preacher has some deep-seated disturbance, together with dissipated urgency and mounting despair. His pulpit is like a certain house at Newport, whose function has changed: no longer a place for exciting parties, it has become a shrine visited by the uncommitted.

The Recovery of Self-Esteem

Hence the question arises for the minister, "What am I doing in the pulpit?" "What is my task?" "Should I keep at it?" "What is my *raison d'être?*" For the answers to all these questions we are forced back to the consideration of religious imagination. The power to see, and to see for others, is the essence of preaching. The power to see current happenings in connection with Scripture happenings, to see behind the ephemeral to God, to proclaim a saving word with an "other side" quality, makes this vocation relevant and important. The ability to be surprised by an insight, to cry "Eureka!" at a new gospel relevance, has power for the minister even before an encounter with a congregation. That ability is the atmosphere of another world that some part of his or her own personality needs to stay alive. If that power leaves, the preacher's life becomes a vacant house open for vandals. If the power stays, the preacher's vocation is still a habitat. And what is life for the preacher is life for the hearer. For those whose creativity is in other important but secular fields, the need is the same. Man does not live by bread alone, even when the bread is made from an unusual recipe. Life is always sustained from the other side, and not from the bustling activities in office and industry. To live and help others live by seeing the deeper dimension in ordinary human affairs, this is the function of the preacher.

Such a preacher is a seer in a great tradition. His or her work is of the same sort as the work of seers within the canon. The function of an Isaiah, an Amos, or a Hosea did not evaporate when the canon was established. It continues past the wall of that canon. By New Testament standards, the Spirit is not an on-again, off-again power. As of this day, it is poured out upon all flesh. Therefore, the same Spirit is stirring up minds to penetrate that ever-present boundary between the finite and the infinite. Every generation walks this boundary, unaware that it exists until it is pointed out. To see it is to take heart and live. To miss it is to crisscross the trail in despair; or, in the language of Jeremiah, to walk the twilight mountains. That is what makes preaching so important. Whether the message seen is a boiling pot from the north or the vine and fig tree of peace, the people at large and the people of God in particular ask the modern preacher, "What do you see?" This is the same question that was directed to Amos. Therefore, the canonical seer and the modern seer are soul brothers. Their function is the same and, in all probability, their manner of receiving the message is the same.

The manner of receiving the inspiration and working it through creatively is the strange common denominator of the entire creative process. Not only do Biblical prophets have ties to latter-day prophets, but both of these religious seers have ties to all seers in all walks of life. Years ago, Rudolf Otto pointed out similar psychological/metaphysical feelings that all people have *vis-à-vis* the divine. There was, according to Otto, the "idea of the holy," with its concomitant effect of holy mystery. But why limit that to the holy, with its connotations of

Biblical, Judeo-Christian faith? A strange similarity of experience binds all who participate in the creative process. Abraham Maslow, who uses the term "peak experience" to describe inspirations that come, as I have already described, while one is "running up the stairs," also notes how these can be received in all areas, certainly not only the religious or even the artistic. Then, Maslow notes what was a new discovery to him. No matter where people get their "peak experience," their descriptions of the subjective effects are much the same. He writes, "I assure you that it was a startling thing for me to hear a woman describing her feelings as she gave birth to a child in the same words used by Bucke (1923) to describe the 'cosmic consciousness,' or by Huxley to describe the 'mystic experience' in all cultures and eras, or by Ghiselin to describe the creative process, or by Suzuki to describe the Zen *satori* experience."[63] Creativity, at least in its psychological effects, parades under an infinite number of banners.

Preachers stand in two great traditions. If they wish, they can look over the vast field of creative seers in the world today and say, "We are one of these." Or they can easily pass through the doors in the canonical wall and say, in regard to the great apostles and prophets, "We are your kinspeople too." If the world pivots on its seers, then all taken together help the movement. However, many preachers do not sense this importance. As we have indicated, pride in vocation is ebbing among many ministers. Most go through the weekly function of preaching as if it were a tedious chore. Inspiration is buried and silted over. Even the joy of the most creative is turned into a wasteland. What was such an important part of the past, a ministry from the pulpit, is like a mound on an arid stretch, just an indication to archaeologists that the thriving life of a city once lay underneath.

This negative feeling must be reversed. Preachers have reason to throw back their shoulders and stand tall. They need not be mousey in a world that says there are "too many churches and too few chop houses." They should have a good feeling about themselves. Until they do, they will not have much to give to neighbors, to say nothing of what they should give back to God. Too much ancestral self-abasement, together with a modern feeling of uselessness, has squelched the ego strength of ministers. No wonder that for many ministers "the same wheel deepens the same rut year after year." Therefore, we must affirm ourselves, and get up on a solid road that runs bravely into the future. Creativity, the function of seeing and expressing, is the essence of a preaching ministry, and the basis of self-esteem.

Consider, for instance, the importance of the materials we use: words, properly polished and shafted and fitted to ideas. They are vital in any advance along a spiritual frontier. They are not weak, fragile nonsense syllables confronting hard realities. Words might never encase the inspiration, and they may, as Eliot says, "strain, crack and break" under the weight they carry. They may even be substitutes for action, and end up the children of hypocrisy. Yet they can also bless, blast, picture, prod, inspire, infuriate, and trigger other minds to think or act. For instance, what subtle, deft touches are given to the countryside by Robert Frost in that eight-line poem which begins, "I'm going out to clean the pasture spring."[64] He pictures himself stopping to rake the leaves away, and waiting until the water bubbles clear. He concludes: "I sha'n't be gone long.—You come too." The poem functions as an invitation that even a city boy might heed. If, in the preacher's mind, the pasture becomes a Promised Land and is treated winsomely, an effective job of evangelism can take place.

For those locked in city streets with city problems, a vision of a pasture and spring is not bad. If we are surrounded by asphalt streets and high-rise factories and we run to the rhythm of machinery, then someone who can see a better way would be a modern equivalent to the writer of the Twenty-third Psalm—green pastures, still waters, restored souls. If a breather can be found from high-tension wires, high-tension nerves, and tense international relations, then perhaps the journey can be made. Add to this the vision of a new land where righteousness dwells, and put that vision in terms of new laws, fair employment practices, and better housing, and a crowd may start to listen. Words spoken with finesse and informed by gospel hope are not insignificant. They open up a few new directions for those who never see past the city smog. Or they add to our blandness a touch of spice. In an interesting exchange, the dancer-dramatist Diaghilev said to the filmmaker Jean Cocteau: "Well, Jean. *Étonnez-moi!*" ("Astonish me!") That, too, is the province of the preacher's words, to add the touch of spice for those who have tasted enough secular life to know how bland it really is.

However, the word of astonishment or spice must be some word from God. It is not editorial comment nor amusing diversion. It is not even the sympathetic word of a fellow sufferer. William Faulkner, in his acceptance speech after receiving the Nobel Prize for literature, stressed this in a memorable sentence: "It is easy enough to say . . . that when the last ding-dong of doom has clanged and faded from the last worthless rock hanging tideless in the last red and dying evening that even then there will still be one more sound: that of his [man's] puny inexhaustible voice still talking. I refuse to accept this. I believe that man will not merely endure: he will prevail."[65] But this other-than-human word is the gospel we preach, whether for judgment or promise. It is the insight from that intertwined sacred realm for those who already suspect that man shall not live by bread alone.

This word has a strange property. It not only illustrates, it also creates. To understand this distinction in itself enhances the preacher's self-image. For instance, if faith were a series of truths stacked up in some New Testament warehouse, the preacher's task would be one of illustration and update. Simply remove a vital truth from the bin, dust off its archaic language, think of a modern analogy, and drive the truth home in as jazzy a way as possible. This view of preaching suffers from two delusions. First, it makes of truth a series of static commodities, limited in number, already processed and waiting. Second, it makes of the preacher no more than a gospel illustrator, which vocation has about as much appeal to the preacher as painting lampshades had to the young Renoir. The art was simply illustrating, not creating. Preachers are not in the vocation of illustrators, valid though the latter might be. Preachers are creators. Such is the strange power of the words they use. In Genesis, God spoke the world into being. To Isaiah, God said: "My word shall *accomplish* that which I purpose." God's word brings to pass. It creates a new thing. Through the word of Elijah, God spoke, and the rain clouds evaporated. God spoke again, and the sky poured rain.

To visualize this power is not easy. In broad philosophical terms, that which is created has being as over against nonbeing. The preacher in his sermon is trying to cause being to stand forth and be identified as such, all the while feeling that nonbeing or chaos is the mysterious and demonic contender. Perhaps the old metaphysical word "substance" has more picture content than being. The preacher is calling forth that which is firm. He identifies the city which has foundations because his word has already laid the substratum and the footings. He is like the professor who said that in all the maze of the times, he wanted to give his students some small platform on which to stand to see their world. That, too, is substance which is created by the word that is spoken. Archibald MacLeish claims that poetry has this same object, to call forth being in the face of nonbeing. He quotes a Chinese poet: "We poets struggle with nonbeing to force it to yield Being. We knock upon silence for an answering music."[66] That task is not just a reshuffling of clever ideas. It is a struggle in which the firm thing arises out of the very chaos that threatens to undo it. Just so, the preacher, poised like Rodin's *Thinker*, rises with some word of meaning on which someone can stand who might otherwise be carried away. Meaning is firm. It has substance. It does not splinter and fragment. In Biblical terms, such a word of the Lord does not "fall to the ground" the way human words fall and break.

Another way to visualize the creative power of the preacher's word is to look at the life-giving qualities it possesses. Meanings dance off in all directions and touch other minds, which then come alive in their own time and with their own unique capacities. Undoubtedly, the new creations in other minds may be the last such that the preacher would imagine. His faithfulness to his own insight, faithfully proclaimed, has simply revealed the Word, which made the rounds on its own and touched the others to life.

One of the great communicators of our time was the actor Charles Laughton. He tells of visiting Chartres

Cathedral as a young man and being taken around by the elderly curator to see the stained-glass windows. The little man in a bowler hat and with piercing blue eyes was ecstatic about his subject. He insisted Laughton stay over a few days and see those windows at different times, and under various shades of morning and evening light. The experience became part of Laughton's spiritual equipment. Years later, he became fascinated with the paintings of Manessier and then formed a friendship with the painter himself. One day, while Laughton was visiting Manessier in France, the two men decided to take a motor trip to Chartres. On the way, Laughton sensed that the colors he admired in Manessier's paintings were the ones he had seen in the windows—turbulent reds, blues, indigos, streaks of green and amber. With a simple question, Laughton found that Manessier had visited the same windows years before and had met the same little man in the bowler hat. "We've had a good father, you and I," said Laughton. From classic windows through the eye and word of a curator, to a painter and an actor, and thence to the rest of us. That is like the movement of the preacher's creative word. It seems alive and life-giving. It comes out of nothing and is proclaimed in spite of our human inadequacy to see it whole. Even in an imperfect form, it pirouettes, turns, and reaches out a fairy wand over the least suspecting. Substance and life are the identifying marks of the word the preacher proclaims.

These aspects of the word bless the nation as well as the church. They are ways God sends his good things on the just and the unjust. It is not by chance that most leaders in African states, though themselves not necessarily Christian, have grown up in mission schools. Even Nkrumah, an antagonist of the West until his death, used a perversion of a Biblical text for the inscription on his statue: "Seek first the political kingdom, and everything else will be added to you." The word of freedom, if not of rebellion, was fashioned from Biblical soil. It is this word, even where not traced back to the Biblical God, which is the seed that cracks the wall of oppression.

Several observers have pointed out the significance of Russia's crackdown on creativity. Musicians were ordered not to venture into the dissonant sounds and odd rhythms of the new era.[67] Russian artists are encouraged to stick to realism, particularly portraits of heroes and scenes of the Revolution.[68] Poets are not free to express the wide range of thoughts by which they try to make sense of the world. Instead of the freedom to create, a doctrinaire party line of acceptability is put forth as the measuring rod. What exceeds the measure is simply cut off. The critics of Russia point out, and rightly so, that rigid systems cannot tolerate the free flow of ideas that keep springing up from creative people. In this connection, it is significant that Communist Russia from its inception has tried to subdue the church. Has this suppression been caused by the sluggish, reactionary attitude of the church, its league with the Czar, its pie-in-the-sky mentality, its preference for the *status quo?* Or, is it quite the reverse? Is there an explosive quality to Christian faith that will not tolerate intolerance? Does the new word in each new age knock against conformity, battling it with a two-edged sword? If not in Russia, at least in Africa, South America, and our own history, the Word of the Lord has been substance and life of a new order, which is brought forth precariously on the borderland between ancient wrongs and future abyss.

But now let us focus on the minister as a person. Grant the truth that what he or she sees has substance and gives life. Accept for the moment the truth that the world needs a Word from God that performs the Jeremiah function of breaking down and building up. Give approval to the ancient proverb that where there is no vision the people perish. The important thing is that involvement in producing that vision has positive effects on the minister. The process of seeing has its own rewards. Let us list some of these.

Rewards for the Seer

1. *A New Sense of Creation.* Throughout this book, we have assumed that creativity in all walks of life is the moving force toward a new heaven and a new earth. Whether or not the apocalyptic strand in the Bible is correct, and some great cataclysm and Second Coming will usher in the new age, makes no matter. The sudden appearance of a new heaven and a new earth will still be a creation, and therefore in keeping with the creativity that manifests itself around the globe in geniuses as well as in common folk. It may be, as Maslow suggests, that a first-rate soup has more creativity than a second-rate painting. The higher truth is that cooks and painters are involved in a creative process that extends over a wide frontier. The minister sees this and proclaims the glory of humanity to the glory of God. He ranges over the world in his mind to find new material for psalms of praise. His God, who has previously been known at Sinai and Calvary, is no small God. This fact itself calls for a prophet within the Christian family who can throw open the church windows to the world. Unfortunately, with the great knowledge explosion, the church has suffered, and the minister along with it. Either the church has grown more provincial, and simply "revved up" the motor of old songs and stale ideas, or it has succumbed to the prevail-

ing opinion that the gospel is irrelevant to modern times. In the first case, the world sees the church walking backward over a sawdust trail. In the second, the world listens in vain for a saving word. To be able to stand in the Biblical tradition; to own allegiance to the God of Abraham, Isaac, and Jacob, as well as to the God and Father of our Lord Jesus Christ; and still to salute all creativity—this is a faith that can embrace the world. No minister can be small-minded when everything in the creation is holy ground.

God's creation and human creativity are very close. This is what the seer sees. Perhaps, to use old theological terms, anthropology and soteriology are intertwined. From the baby in a crib who discovers his hand, to a scientist who discovers a vaccine, to a senior citizen who discovers a new skill, we are always responding to God's call. That is our nature which God has placed within and which, when called forth, produces fulfillment. Those who do not create something, even first-rate soup, are not alive. Man is *homo creator.* Sin is the rebellion, pride, guilt, and whatever else, that blocks us from our true nature. The cross is the forgiveness of sin, the promise of resurrection, the release to new life as creators. We are called to be new creations in Christ Jesus. We are constantly made alive by expressing that life as creators. Nothing God created is static. God's creation has the movement of a Van Gogh sky or cypress garden. To see this, to see that creation and creativity are linked, adds breadth and stature to the one who sees.

It is unfortunate that we preachers do not say clearly that God and man are linked in creativity. We talk about God's intervention in human life, but we seldom stress our response in terms of creativity. Usually, the response is some form of faithful submission rather than innovation. It is as if God does all the thinking in the big office while we are on the assembly line or maintenance crew. Thus man is tender of the garden, receiver of the law, interpreter of a word which he has no part in fashioning, participant in the body of Christ where the thinking is already done. All these descriptions of man's role have truth, but they underplay the human agency to make the point that all is of God.

Without denying that all is of God, we must stress that our power as creators is the break-in point for so much of what God is doing in his world. It is this power which gives distinction to the word "human." It is through the breaking in of creative power that we tend the garden until it brings forth miracle wheat, or that we become instruments of righteousness in a specific case of social action. The body of Christ interacts with the world through the creative insights we receive from the head, but which we must work through as laboriously as any researcher tracking down hypotheses. If the terms we use to speak of God and of humanity cover up the surging creativity in either, they have hidden what may be the essential element in life. But if, on the other hand, creativity is identified, then as with Brother Lawrence, the whole universe can become our place of prayer. Not only will the seer be a cosmopolitan Christian, but he or she might also make it possible for some engineer or lawyer to leave the far country of secular creativity and come back to the Father's house, the party, and the dance.

2. *A New Sense of Freedom.* No one is free who has a scribe mentality, and no one is free who is so disconnected from tradition that he floats all over the place. The former slavishly repeats the past with a jot-and-tittle faith-

fulness. The latter is the product of the last book read, or
the victim of the latest fad, blown about by every wind
of doctrine. Of course, rigid traditionalists gain in security
what they lose in freedom. They know in advance what
the Word of the Lord is. They hope not to be victimized
by change, and to keep the faith. On the other hand,
those disconnected from tradition gain a supposed freedom, so that they never have to apologize for an ancient
creed or unpopular ethic. They dance loose from that.
But neither of them is really free. The former people are
embedded in tradition like fossils. The latter float like
milkweed. T. S. Eliot described the latter when he said,
"Most people think they are free when they have only
come unbuttoned."

Real freedom has to contain the paradox of being
bound and loose at the same time. Of knowing and not
knowing. Of having it nailed down and constantly coming loose. Of being slaves to Christ and yet free. Imagination meets the paradox head on and accepts it. Seers have
the gospel story as a dominant motif, but the story is not
presented as footnotes to a doctoral thesis. The story is
in the body of the text, reworked to apply to the issues
at hand. Seers take the Bible seriously but not woodenly.
They have made the story their own, re-presenting it in
new times and for new occasions. They have the security
only of knowing that what they have said is authentic,
that it comes from the mystic center of their lives. However, the security is a constant process, always arriving,
never having arrived. Because they are bound to what
God has already done and open to what God is wanting
to do, seers stay on the growing edge of God's purposes.
They are not blown all over the map, neither are they
nailed down in one place. "The past is prologue," and in
an active way, seers use their imaginative powers to pic-

ture for themselves and others the shape of the prologue. That is freedom in a new and vital sense.

Aaron Copland has some interesting parallels to the preacher's task when he speaks of the relation of the composer to the performer.[69] An orchestra conductor, for instance, is bound to the score in the same way as a minister-preacher is bound to the Scriptures. Both are in trouble if they don't know the score. Yet both are free to be themselves in relation to that score. Copland points out that it is impossible to put all the notations on music that would permit an exact reproduction of the composer's intention. There is not the similarity between the score and the composer's mind that there is between a photograph and the subject. Copland acknowledges that the music he writes is capable of many interpretations, else it could not be great music. He comments that Paul Rosenfeld visualized steel frames when he heard *Piano Variations.* Just so, the English critic Wilfred Mellera found in the final movement of the *Piano Sonata* "a quintessential musical expression of the idea of immobility." The critic went on to say, "The music runs down like a clock and dissolves away into eternity." "Fine that they should think this about these pieces," says Copland, "but these ideas were farthest from my mind when I wrote the music." If a composer feels that way about his music—both that he couldn't possibly put down all that is in his mind, and that he appreciates the enlarged meaning that other interpretations give—how can God be of less a mind, both in doing his mighty acts, and then in allowing a wide interpretation of them?

The great themes of Exodus and Calvary have their notations, and they are meant to be played repeatedly, but the ways of seeing and playing these are legion. When Moses and Elijah on the Mount of Transfiguration spoke of the "exodus" which Jesus would accomplish at Jerusalem, that is one way. When Leon Uris spoke of "exodus" in a novel, that is another, a secular, expression. A grosser form of expression is that of Cecil B. De Mille. A finer interpretation was that of Martin Luther King, relating the exodus to modern liberation from slavery. Each one sees the score from a new perspective and with a new set of eyes. That is not only an option that the interpreter has, it is a necessity. Copland decries those who woodenly try to play the score. "Nothing is so boring as a well-rehearsed performance; well rehearsed in the sense that nothing can be expected to happen except what is studiously prepared in advance. . . . A live performance should be just that—live to all the incidents that happen along the way, colored by the subtle nuances of momentary emotions, inspired by the sudden insights of public communication."[70] That advice would fit the Scripture interpreter too. Neither preaches a wooden jot-and-tittle proclamation nor a private ditty that has no relation to the Scriptures. The idea is faithfulness to the score and your own interpretation of the score.

With that freedom, no passage of Scripture should sound as though it belonged totally back in the first century. If it does, then leave it alone until some modern sounds start to be heard. Many Scriptures lie dormant for long periods until some change of style or experience brings out the divine "Aha!" deep inside. For instance, the apocalyptic element, with imminent disaster, unusual natural phenomena, final battle, Second Coming, has not been popular in mainline preaching. However, when war intrudes, or nuclear holocaust is imminent, or "future shock" dawns, then the poetry of the Apocalypse takes on a realism it did not have before. The apocalyptic music is played with new urgency and meaning. How appropri-

ate are these lines of William Butler Yeats, built on New
Testament imagery, but turned to the modern scene:

> Turning and turning in the widening gyre,
> The falcon cannot hear the falconer;
> Things fall apart; the centre cannot hold;
> Mere anarchy is loosed upon the world.
> . . . .
> Surely some revelation is at hand;
> Surely the Second Coming is at hand.
> The Second Coming! Hardly are those words out
> When a vast image out of *Spiritus Mundi*
> Troubles my sight: somewhere in sands of the desert
> A shape with lion body and the head of a man,
> A gaze blank and pitiless as the sun,
> Is moving its slow thighs, while all about it
> Reel shadows of the indignant desert birds.
> The darkness drops again; but now I know
> That twenty centuries of stony sleep
> Were vexed to nightmare by a rocking cradle,
> And what rough beast, its hour come round at last,
> Slouches towards Bethlehem to be born?[71]

To play a Biblical score this way is the freedom and
grandeur, to say nothing of the usefulness, of the Christian seer.

3. *A New Sense of Self-Worth and Identity.* One modern preacher-theologian who runs a center for continuing
education observed that most of the ministers he interviewed did not have the ego strength to crush a fly, let
alone fight dragons. Ego strength comes from knowing
who you are and why you are here. At the risk of repetition, let me say that both these questions are getting
harder for ministers to answer. They look at other vocations with some envy, because the work in them looks

more definite and rewarding. The doctor operates, the dentist drills, the lawyer argues cases, and they all get well paid. What does a minister do? The situation is made more complex because in changing times, all the former foundations for ministry become debatable. It used to be that the minister "saved souls." Now the phrase has too many connotations of sawdust trails, buttonhole evangelism, and simplistic theology to give much support to the average minister. Does he or she then practice the "cure of souls" in the old sense of Richard Baxter or Jeremy Taylor? Once again, the new day puts that function more often with the psychiatrist or secular counselor. Is the minister then a social reformer of the Rauschenbusch or Gladden tradition? Perhaps, but many political figures are more sensitive to society's needs and twice as effective in working with the power structure. Well, perhaps the old title "preacher" will give the modern minister some identity. Yet not too many ministers would feel complimented by the title. It is no wonder the modern minister is bewildered. That is when the Willy Loman epitaph is revisited and the lines become personal. "Poor Rev. Loman, he didn't know who he was."

What is the minister? He or she is a seer. What do ministers do? They constantly exercise their God-given imagination on all the material that takes center stage in their minds. Are they needed? More than they know. Are they appreciated? Not necessarily; at least the appreciation does not always show in salary or community deference. Why don't they forget it? They can't. The vision commands as it seeks expression through them. Is it enough to be a seer? Yes. The vision puts the minister's life in touch constantly with the behind-the-scenes aspect of reality. It commands and leads him or her out into the wilderness in search of the meaning of things, and to report the findings to others. The process is near to what Paul means by being a person "in Christ"; one who possesses the "mind of Christ"; one who knows the anguish of "seeing through a glass, darkly" and the ecstasy of being able to put some things together. There is something ennobling about the process. It delivers the minister from "Milquetoastism."

The results are not quite as irrelevant as many ministers think. What grays the lives of most parishioners is not red-blooded sins so much as boredom, dullness, the inability to see beyond the next bill or paycheck. In this context, the minister accepts the challenge of Auden: "Redeem for the dull the Average Way, that common ungifted natures may believe that their normal vision can walk to perfection."[72] This is the big purpose the minister is about. In the bargain, it gives him or her that O.K. feeling inside. The questions are answered, "Who am I?" "What am I here to do?"

This assumes that ministers accept the role of seer. They need not. There are so many prepackaged visions, carefully indexed and ready for instant use. Prayers, sermons, programs, ticky-tacky paste-ups. The use of these is one way ministers sell their souls for a mess of pottage. There are other ways nearly as bad. The minister can become a scholarly "yes person." This type loads up a sermon with literary and technical quotes. This preacher exerts some imagination, true, but ends up more like an artisan than a visionary. Imagination does not disparage scholarship, Biblical or otherwise. But it draws upon scholarship suggestively for its own independent purposes, and what it presents, it transforms. Such imagination puts its material through labor pains so that it can bring forth a new creation—in this case, a sermon worth listening to.

Ministers who are willing to be seers have the worth of being for real. They know that what they are producing week by week is their own, even if not of heroic proportions. They do not need false supports for their ego: How much salary do I get? How much power? What size congregation? Also, they are free from the fear of the younger generation coming up and walking all over their ambitions. Like Plato's philosopher-king, who is not fit to rule until at least fifty years of age, the modern prophet-seer may be seeing things more deeply at fifty than at thirty. He may not have comparable energy to crank the mimeograph and run to every meeting in town. However, too often physical energy has been confused with effectiveness. When that happens, aging is always a threat. What is needed is not more energy in the minister, but a vision that can release it in others. That being so, the imaginative power, plus the accompanying feeling of self-worth, need not deteriorate with age. As Joel said, and Peter repeated,"Your young men shall see visions, and your old men shall dream dreams."

4. *A New Sense of the Holy Spirit's Work.* There seems to be in our time a renewed interest in the Holy Spirit. This is seen in the Pentecostal movements in all denominations as well as in the call for renewal that has occupied most churches. The problem is this: how can we put intelligent meaning into our desire? Either we end up with the Scylla of intellectualism, an enlarged *doctrine* of the Holy Spirit, or else we are on the Charybdis of emotional sentimentalism. One sharpens the mind, the other titillates the spirit, but neither gets very close to the marketplace of life. For instance, any theological book will have a chapter or two on the person and work of the Holy Spirit; however, the subject described is as much

like the reality as an essay on da Vinci is comparable to standing before the *Mona Lisa.* A doctrine of the Spirit is almost an anomaly. However, to move in the direction of emotion in describing the Spirit leads to the opposite excess. Whether you observe the iconoclastic movement of Carlstadt and some of Luther's associates, or get caught up in the joy syndrome of some of the Jesus people, the end product is usually a heightening of the spirit with a lessening of intellectual direction. Motors run without gears being engaged. How can the dilemma be avoided?

The problem is further complicated by the vagueness of the term "Holy Spirit." We have vital images of God the Father. We have a concrete historical figure of Jesus of Nazareth. The Spirit is a different matter. The symbols of fire and wind, though useful, do not in themselves point as easily to a reality behind them as the symbols of Father or Savior. We grasp the symbols of the Spirit more in terms of psychological effects—enthusiasm, joy, refreshment, etc.—than as transcendental reality.

There is another problem when anyone thinks about the Holy Spirit. Much of the Biblical language of the Spirit is easily transferred into language about the Father or the Son. When Jesus says that the Spirit will not speak of himself, but "will take what is mine and declare it to you" (John 16:14), he seems to transpose Spirit talk into talk about himself. Similarly, does it really matter if we say that the Spirit convicts persons of sin (John 16:8), or if we say Jesus does that? Does the Spirit bring Ezekiel's valley of dry bones to life, or is that simply a shorthand way of speaking about the power of God the Father? Paul can speak about the Holy Spirit or the Spirit of Christ almost interchangeably (compare Rom. 8:9 with Rom. 8:26). If everything we say about the Spirit can be transposed, the implication is that the Holy Spirit is simply a synonym for God the Father or God the Son. This is, of course, to talk in an unsophisticated way. But practically speaking, how do you solve the problem of conversing about the Spirit when it seems like grabbing a handful of air?

One answer is to use the language of creativity insofar as that language rests on the Biblical revelation. The Spirit may be the power in the center of personality that makes us seers into the nature and purposes of God. It —or He—or She (perhaps She, especially since creation and the arts have usually been described in mythology as feminine)—is the activator of imagination. The Spirit is the womb where thought originates and is nourished and finally born. As Paul said, "What no eye has seen, nor ear heard . . . God has revealed to us through the Spirit" (II Cor. 2:9–10).

To say that the Spirit is the power within us to see is not to reach outside the Bible for a metaphor. The opening of Genesis pictures the Spirit brooding over the primordial chaos preparatory to the work of creation. It is the ordering force before the first word of God, "Let there be light." Jesus promised that the creation would continue to happen by the Spirit. We would be "born of the Spirit"; we would do greater works than the apostolic band and unfold teaching that Jesus left undeveloped, all by the Spirit. In such passages, the later disciples, people like ourselves, are to extend the activity of God outside the canon just as we have observed God's activity inside the canon. It is the work of the Holy Spirit to drive the imaginative power of Christians toward the boundary between the finite and the eternal, the old creation and the new, where we have been and where God wants us to be now.

This must be a pilgrimage. What was progress and innovative thinking for the last generation may be dry bones for our own. What was vital in the Bible, and that which nurtures our faith and informs our vision, is open-ended. The ancient verities call for reinterpretation, so as to show another side of their many facets. No single statement, however insightful, is adequate once the occasion for the insight is past. It is not that the Biblical word of judgment is being fulfilled: "ever learning, and never able to come to the knowledge of the truth." Rather, it is the Biblical word of promise, "You shall see greater things than these." The tradition keeps spiraling outward from the creative source in Jesus, in a movement that is always connected to the incarnation, always fuller in its outer turns, but never complete.

Jesus suggested movement in the truth he revealed, even in the title he chose for himself, "the Way." Ways are roads. They cut through valleys, wind around mountains, parallel railroads and rivers, enter cities, find the passes in mountains and disappear over the horizon. Roads are not destinations. They are the ways to get there. Roads suggest pilgrimage, travel, movement, restlessness, the need to get on to the next stopover. Paul expressed this late in his life when he confessed: "I do not consider myself to have 'arrived,' spiritually. . . . But I keep going on . . ." (Phil. 3:12, 14, Phillips). Or again, "Forgetting what lies behind and straining forward to what lies ahead, I press on . . ." That is the attitude of pilgrimage, the mind-set of the seer-preacher. That is the guarantee of freshness in exchange for faithfulness, so that we will not go stale in one secure position. There is no secure position. Something inside says, "Keep moving on."

It is noteworthy that this restlessness keeps popping up

as a mark on the mind of creative people. Thomas Mann, near the end of the meditations that introduce his story of *Joseph and His Brothers,* revealed the feeling:

As for me, who now draw my narrative to a close, . . . I will not conceal my native and comprehensive understanding of the old man's restless unease and dislike of any fixed abode. For, do not I know the feeling? To me, too, has not unrest been ordained, have not I too been endowed with a heart which knows not repose? The story teller's story—is it not the moon, lord of the road, the wanderer, who moves in his stations, one after another, freeing himself from each? For the story teller makes many a station, roving and relating, but pauses only tent-wise, awaiting further directions, and soon feels his heart beating high, partly with desire, partly too from fear and anguish of the flesh, but in any case, as a sign that he must take the road toward fresh adventures which are to be painstakingly lived through, down to their remotest details, according to the restless Spirit's will.[73]

The preacher feels this, too. He or she could write the same language, and feel the pull of the same star, and the lure of the same road. The mark of restlessness is imprinted on our minds. But it is not the mark of the beast, and the wandering is not "east of Eden." Rather, it is the mark of the Spirit, which promises life along with the movement, and which gives brief glimpses of spires away at the world's rim. There is no escape from restlessness as we make our way from God to God, and describe sights and sounds along the route.

From the personal experience of pilgrimage, and the delight of the journey, we link the Holy Spirit with the function of seeing. To connect but not limit the Spirit to the imagination has many advantages. It explains the mysterious origins of so many of our ideas. It accounts for the sense of a collaborating Other that Robert Louis

Stevenson described. It puts our mini-creations in context with the constant creative activity of God. It allows for the high-pitched emotion—agony or ecstasy, fire or wind —without divorcing emotion from intellect. In the imagination, ancient tradition comes alive, intellect gets the dust blown from it, dry bones take on flesh and walk around. Furthermore, as with all work of the imagination, the aim is to communicate and, if possible, to motivate. It is not imagination run wild, totally subjective, emotion for emotion's sake. The Spirit in mankind is a creative Spirit from God, for the purpose of God's people.

There is a further advantage in seeing imagination as a gift of the Spirit. It properly locates the minister's authority. Where does authority reside in a day when all authority is suspect? The authority is not "out there," external to the minister, for we are not in a mood to submit on that basis. Neither is it "up there"—a God who functions like some Louis XIV of the heavens. The authority is not the Bible as a trim and confident record, for that would locate authority "back there" and still external to us. No, the authority must be internal without being totally subjective. It must be the deep calling to the deep. Somewhere in the mysterious center of the minister's life is the life of the Spirit brooding over what otherwise would be a chaos, allowing the man or woman of God to speak so that "he who has ears" can hear.

5. *A New Power to Motivate.* The minister-preacher would like to turn as many as possible toward God. His or her function is not to bask in private visions, but to point in the direction of what God is doing, and to hope others will follow the finger. It is God who gives sight to the blind and strength to the lame. The ultimate miracle is not within the sermon, but with God who operates,

often through the word we preach. Furthermore, since to see is not to do, the hearer must reshuffle some drives so that new ambitions come out on top. That shuffle is repentance, and that too is God's miracle. Then, we can hope, others will step out on faith, claim the vision as their own, see for themselves. As the citizens of the town said to the woman of Samaria, "It is no longer because of your words that we believe, for we have heard for ourselves, and we know that this is indeed the Savior of the world" (John 4:42). That is the preacher's fervent wish for all who hear; and that too rests on the willingness of God to come fresh to everyone. Yet, granted all this, there are two factors, both related to the imagination, which are often ingredients of the miracle. One is the power of the vivid to motivate, the other is the power of the authentic life.

A seer does not produce the vision for the sake of moving crowds in any Elmer Gantry fashion. Yet, the fact remains, people act more fully and with deeper conviction when they can see. This is why great oratory is always splashed with picture language. Political programs likewise are forceful to the extent that they capture the imagination. Logic can be precise and hard prose can cover all aspects of the topic without ever affecting the will of the hearer. Things remain as they were. However, when Mark Antony appeals to the bloody wounds of Caesar, or Augustine to the *City of God,* or Martin Luther to *The Babylonian Captivity of the Church,* great masses of people get ready to move. This simple fact is known by modern people, else they wouldn't talk about a "chicken in every pot," a "New Deal," "Great Society," "Peace Corps," and the like. The world runs on symbols, slogans, and imaginative programs. Once again, and in a

wider sense, "Where there is no vision, the people perish."

That being so, the Christian minister as seer can be one
of the most forceful persons in the community, by God's
help. The symbols that we deal with—the manger, the
cross, the empty tomb—rest on history and the mighty
acts of God. Vital contact with them not only positions
life at the cosmic center of the things, but gives the seer
something to say that may yet capture the imagination of
the world. The secret is in the mystery of God on the one
hand and the willingness of the seer to labor as any
creative artist, so that the finished product, the sermon,
comes as close as possible to the original impulse that
prompted it.

But more than this is needed. The person who speaks
for God must be an authentic person. There is in Hindu
scripture a familiar refrain whereby the centuries-old material is transmitted. The refrain is, "Thus have I heard."
Of course, those who read these scriptures can do so
simply as scribes, repeating the ancient formula "Thus
have I heard" in wooden, legalistic fashion, but never
grasping the spirit of the teaching that follows. One of
the Hindu anecdotes tries to point out this foible and
show the need for an authentic, up-to-date grasp of the
scripture. The story is told of a conversation between a
guru and his pupil.

GURU: Ananda, do you know the sacred scriptures?
STUDENT: Yes, master, I have been studying them.
GURU: And, do you know the phrase, "Thus have I heard"?
STUDENT: Oh, yes. That is throughout the scriptures.
GURU: Ananda, what have *you* heard?

In the preaching process, that is always the question we
ask ourselves. What have *we* heard? It is a question that

troubles as much as it blesses once the hearing happens. The "voice" comes in snatches. It is not always heard clearly. When it is heard, its transmission is only approximate. This troubles the preacher-seer as much as it troubles any creative person in any discipline. Giacometti, pacing the floor because he can't get the portrait painted just right, or James Baldwin, snapping pencils and kicking the wastebasket because he can't quite put something into words—both know, along with the preacher, that the deeper mystery will never be entirely captured. The only thing worse would be to have the voices go silent, and to be resigned to a dull, three-dimensional world. So, the minister, as in the case of all creative people, waits and struggles to express. Nothing is locked up in tight categories or known in finality. Yet this posture of knowing and not knowing, of seeing through a glass darkly and on some days not at all, has more power to persuade than a safe argument. Those who convey the attitude that the scroll with the seven seals has been opened privately in their presence are not dealing with the same mysteries that trouble most of humanity. The hearing belongs to those who see, and struggle with seeing; who collect their visions and share them like manna one day at a time.

This means that the preacher is always in the process of becoming. His or her essence is never firm like earth, air, fire, and water. Rather, it is in constant movement like the elements in the philosophy of Heraclitus. The blessing to the minister is self-discovery—a progressive answer to the age-old question, "Who am I?" Aaron Copland, in answering the question of why he composed, replied simply that he had to. He had the same necessity as Niagara Falls to spill over. Yet he goes on to say that every composition was a new self-expression, which makes evident one's deepest feelings about life. "I create to know who I am."[74] In this same connection, Copland quotes Jacques Maritain: "It is the artist's condition to seize obscurely his own being with a knowledge that will not come to anything save in being creative, and which will not be conceptualized save in a work made by his own hands."[75]

The minister-preacher is engaged in that same quest of self-discovery. The quest is a never-ending one. The insights are partial. Each gives the message: not yet—more to come. The minister is not the same at middle age as in seminary days, nor as he or she will be. Ministers are persons moving progressively toward a deeper revelation of who they are. Yet it is not simply self-discovery, a gritty command that one gives to oneself to keep on going. The changing power, and the commanding power—that which opens up ourselves to ourselves—is none other than the gospel message we are fervently trying to apprehend. The never-ending, transforming power is God's doing, not our own. Jung once observed: "The work in process becomes the poet's fate and determines his psychic development. It is not Goethe who creates Faust, but Faust which creates Goethe."[76] To paraphrase this, it is not that we create our visions or our self-development, but that our visions are creating us. Christ is being formed in us. "It does not yet appear what we shall be, but we know . . . we shall be like him" (I John 3:2).

The quiet confidence that things are happening to us as we go along gives the plus in preaching for those who preach. If the vision tarries, we wait for it. When it comes, we struggle to present it. That is our life and our becoming. But just as important, our exposure to the process, our honesty with what we don't know as well as our convictions about what we do, is the most powerful persuasion to those who listen and who are battling the same life, with the same need to make sense, eternal sense, out of what confronts them. The power to motivate is strangely attached to the incomplete vision and the struggle to proclaim it which occupies the length of our professional life.

Therefore, if anyone asks us preachers who we are, we respond that we are seers. It is a great vocation with a long tradition. Apart from this function, we haven't much to offer. Certainly, our past sermons haven't much life. They were adequate at the time, but no longer. Now they are solidified visions, cold and lifeless. We cannot live on those, nor can our congregations. Tomorrow's sermons are too far around the corner to be seen, nor can they be written far in advance. We hope that when we get there, we will see some new things which "God has prepared for those who love him."

Meanwhile we live in the today by every word that proceeds from the mouth of God—which we receive in momentary outcroppings of insight. If we live by that word, perhaps we can tell it in such a way that others will live too. But then, having told it, we need to move on. Never to possess. To enjoy, but not to keep. To see. To touch lightly. To be thankful, and then to move on.

NOTES

1. Stephen Spender, "The Making of a Poem," in *Creativity*, ed. P. E. Vernon (Penguin Books, Inc., 1970), p. 74.

2. D. Bruce Lockerbie, *The Liberating Word: Art and the Mystery of the Gospel* (Wm. B. Eerdmans Publishing Co., 1974), p. 34.

3. Rollo May, "The Nature of Creativity," in *Creativity and Its Cultivation*, ed. Harold H. Anderson (Harper & Brothers, 1959), p. 59.

4. From a letter by W. A. Mozart. E. Holmes, *The Life of Mozart, Including His Correspondence* (Chapman & Hall, 1878), pp. 211–213.

5. A. E. Housman, "The Name and Nature of Poetry," in *The Creative Process*, ed. Brewster Ghiselin (University of California Press, 1952), pp. 90–91.

6. *Ibid.*

7. Stanley Rosner and Lawrence E. Abt, *The Creative Experience* (Grossman Publishers, Inc., 1970), p. 37.

8. Rollo May, *The Courage to Create* (W. W. Norton & Co., Inc., 1975), p. 81, taken from James Lord, *A Giacometti Portrait* (Doubleday & Company, Inc., 1965), p. 26.

9. *Ibid.*, p. 83.

10. *Ibid.*

11. Edmund W. Sinnott, "The Creativeness of Life," in Anderson, *Creativity and Its Cultivation*, p. 24.

12. Francis Thompson, "The Kingdom of God." James Dalton Morrison (ed.), *Masterpieces of Religious Verse* (Harper & Brothers, 1948), p. 447.

13. Sam Keen, *To a Dancing God* (Harper & Row, Publishers, Inc., 1970), pp. 22–23.

14. May, *The Courage to Create,* p. 52.

15. *Ibid.,* p. 54.

16. W. F. Ogburn and D. Thomas, "Are Inventions Inevitable?" *Political Science Quarterly,* Vol. 37 (1922), pp. 83–98.

17. See Rosner and Abt, *The Creative Experience;* Jack D. Summerfield and Lorlyn Thatcher (eds.), *The Creative Mind and Method* (Russell & Russell, Inc., 1964); Ghiselin, *The Creative Process;* Eliot D. Hutchinson, *How to Think Creatively* (Abingdon-Cokesbury Press, 1949)—among others.

18. Hutchinson, *How to Think Creatively,* p. 15.

19. *Ibid.,* p. 134.

20. *Ibid.,* p. 165.

21. Dorothy Sayers, *The Mind of the Maker* (Harcourt, Brace & Co., 1941).

22. *Ibid.,* pp. 38–40.

23. *Ibid.,* p. 30.

24. From Huston Smith, *The Religions of Man* (Harper & Brothers, 1958), p. 23.

25. Romain Rolland, *Musicians of To-Day,* tr. by M. Blaiklock (1915); quoted in Hutchinson, *How to Think Creatively,* p. 65.

26. Erich Fromm, "The Creative Attitude," in Anderson, *Creativity and Its Cultivation,* p. 53.

27. For a scholarly study of the terms *nabhi'* and *ro'eh,* prophet and seer, and the reasons why these are two terms for the same person, see H. H. Rowley, *The Servant of the Lord* (London: Lutterworth Press, 1952), pp. 99ff.

28. See Albert C. Sundberg, Jr., "The Bible Canon and the Christian Doctrine of Inspiration," *Interpretation,* Oct. 1975, pp. 352–371.

29. *Ibid.,* p. 371.

30. Gerhard von Rad, *Old Testament Theology,* tr. by D. M. G. Stalker, Vol. II (Harper & Row, Publishers, Inc., 1965), p. 334.

31. For an excellent discussion of true vs. false prophecy, see James L. Crenshaw, *Prophetic Conflict* (Walter de Gruyter, Inc., 1971), pp. 49ff.

32. Rowley, *The Servant of the Lord,* p. 125 (italics his).

33. Ghiselin, *The Creative Process,* p. 66.

34. *Ibid.*

35. Allen Tate, "On Poetry," in Summerfield and Thatcher, *The Creative Mind and Method*, p. 68.

36. Ghiselin, *The Creative Process*, p. 6.

37. Rosner and Abt, *The Creative Experience*, p. 272.

38. Peter Drucker, *The Effective Executive* (Harper & Row, Publishers, Inc., 1966), pp. 25–51.

39. S. T. Coleridge, "Prefatory Note to Kubla Khan." Ghiselin, *The Creative Process*, p. 84.

40. Peter H. McKellar, *Imagination and Thinking* (Basic Books, Inc., Publishers, 1957), p. 124.

41. *Ibid.*, p. 125.

42. Van Gogh, "Letter to Anton Ridder van Rappard." Ghiselin, *The Creative Process*, p. 46.

43. Paul Hindemith, *A Composer's World* (Doubleday & Company, Inc., Anchor Books, 1961), p. 69.

44. Aaron Copland, *Music and Imagination* (Harvard University Press, 1952), pp. 17–18.

45. On January 26, 1975, a group of social activists, among them Richard Neuhaus, William Sloane Coffin, and Peter Berger, issued a proclamation that caught newspaper headlines because it seemed out of character with its authors' previous position. It affirmed the reality of the supernatural and called for a more pious awareness of the Almighty.

46. See article by Francine duPlessix Gray, "To March or Not to March," *The New York Times Magazine*, June 27, 1976, p. 34.

47. Robert Penn Warren, "On Writing," in Summerfield and Thatcher, *The Creative Mind and Method*, p. 60.

48. Christian Zervos, "Conversation with Picasso," in Ghiselin, *The Creative Process*, p. 48.

49. *Ibid.*, p. 51.

50. Copland, *Music and Imagination*, p. 43.

51. Ben Shahn, "The Biography of a Painting," in *Creativity in the Arts*, ed. V. Thomas (Prentice-Hall, Inc., 1964), p. 21.

52. Hindemith, *A Composer's World*, p. 88.

53. *Ibid.*, p. 70.

54. These three examples are in McKellar, *Imagination and Thinking*, p. 119.

55. Henri Poincaré, "Mathematical Creation," in Ghiselin, *The Creative Process*, p. 25.

56. May, *The Courage to Create*, p. 66.

57. T. Sharper Knowlson, *Originality: A Popular Study of the Creative Mind* (Werner & Laurie, 1917), p. 87.

58. Hutchinson, *How to Think Creatively*, p. 81.

59. Warren, "On Writing," in Summerfield and Thatcher, *The Creative Mind and Method*, p. 6.

60. Abraham Maslow, "Creativity in Self-Actualizing People," in Anderson, *Creativity and Its Cultivation*, p. 86.

61. Carl R. Rogers, "Toward a Theory of Creativity," *ibid.*, pp. 75f.

62. *Ibid.*

63. Maslow, "Creativity in Self-Actualizing People," in Anderson, *Creativity and Its Cultivation*, p. 89.

64. Robert Frost, "The Pasture," *Collected Poems* (Halcyon House, 1930), p. 1.

65. *The Faulkner Reader* (Random House, Inc., 1954), p. 4.

66. Archibald MacLeish, *Poetry and Experience* (Houghton Mifflin Company, 1961), pp. 8f.

67. See Copland, *Music and Imagination*, p. 76.

68. The author viewed a traveling exhibit of Russian paintings on loan to the National Museum of Bucharest. Of fifty paintings, all were portraits except for one scene of Tolstoy walking in his garden and another of Lenin on his balcony surrounded by red flags.

69. Copland, *Music and Imagination*, pp. 49ff.

70. *Ibid.*, p. 52.

71. William Butler Yeats, "The Second Coming," *Collected Poems* (The Macmillan Company, 1956).

72. W. H. Auden, "For the Time Being," *Collected Longer Poems* (Random House, Inc., 1969), p. 156.

73. Ghiselin, *The Creative Process*, p. 8.

74. Copland, *Music and Imagination*, p. 40.

75. *Ibid.*

76. *Ibid.*